Lee & Me

WHAT I LEARNED FROM PARENTING A CHILD
WITH ADVERSE CHILDHOOD EXPERIENCES

BY WENDY BORDERS GAUNTNER

"*Lee & Me* provides real-life insight into the challenges *and* triumphs of a true-life 'Trauma Momma,' a term I reserve for adoptive mom's who have mastered the art of Therapeutic Parenting. Becoming an adoptive parent of a child with early adverse experiences can stretch, bend — even break some. Wendy Gauntner's unfettered account of her *own* personal growth through the process of becoming an adoptive mom is a must-read for every parent!

As expected, the voyage of adoption begins with Wendy's unbridled excitement, but quickly shifts to relentless efforts to heal her child's hurting heart, mind, body and soul. Wendy eloquently takes the reader along through the passage of self-doubt, beyond the white-caps of terror and exhaustion, below the waterfall of needing to control, to reach the harbor of healing that — unexpectedly — was for her transformation, not her child's.

Wendy shares her masterful approach to negotiating complex or rigid systems to secure flexible services for her child.

If you are typically inclined to skip over suggestions for self-care, I assure you will not this time. By the time you reach this section, you will already have sensed the shift in her very essence; you will want to know more about how she garnered the inner-wisdom, peace, insight and strength to become a warrior mom — who also soldiers for her own self-care."

DENISE L. BEST M.A., L.P.C., CENTER FOR HEALING RELATIONSHIPS, LLC
Author *"Therapeutic Interventions & Parenting Techniques for Children with Developmental Delays, Attachment & Trauma Disorders"*

"Parenting any child is hard work, but when your child is experiencing life 'just outside the lines,' it's even harder. Here's where Wendy Gauntner's *Lee & Me* comes in, like a good friend, offering equal parts information and understanding. If you don't have a child with Adverse Childhood Experiences (ACES), you probably know one — read this book to better understand the families around you. And if you have a child with ACES, this book is written especially for you. She has given you her story — eloquently, thoughtfully, generously — so that you can know you're not alone."

JENNIFER GRAF GRONEBERG
Author of *Road Map to Holland* (NAL/Penguin 2008) and *My Heart's First Steps: Writings that Celebrate the Gifts of Parenthood* (Adams Media, 2004)

"This is an honest account of one mother's courageous journey through the process of parenting a child with attachment disorder and adverse childhood experience (ACE). The author's description of attachment issues and ACE is detailed in a way that will make it recognizable to parents of affected children, a layperson's truthful and vulnerable description of the attachment-disordered child and the difficulties of parenting that child.

All parents will be comforted by the candor exhibited in this book and all parents will benefit from the reading of this book. However, parents of children with attachment disorder and/or ACE will be especially heartened and hopeful. This mother's journey through the most difficult and painful endeavor, the effort to assist a troubled child in finding his/her way in the world, will assure them that they are not alone.

As a mental health clinician, I was impressed with the author's well-informed translation of attachment theory into everyday language. As a parent, I was moved by the author's bravery and inspired by her perseverance as she struggled to help her child to be "normal" and to heal.

Lee & Me reminds us that loss is inevitable, but also powerfully demonstrates the possibility of healing and growth that lies within each parent and child."

SUSAN C. BALTIMORE

Licensed Clinical Social Worker, Adjunct Faculty (ret.),
UCLA School of Public Policy, Department of Social Welfare

WENDY BORDERS GAUNTNER

Lee & Me

WHAT I LEARNED FROM
PARENTING A CHILD WITH
ADVERSE CHILDHOOD EXPERIENCES

Cover Design: John Matthews

Interior Design: Heidi Miller

Editing: Kate Makled & Grace Kerina

Author's photo courtesy of Michelle Alspaw-English, Shades of Life Photography

DEDICATION

Dedicated to my husband

He has been with me every moment of my journey
and is the unsung hero of our family

Table of Contents

Preface

This is my story.

This story does not belong to my son or my husband, who have equally compelling stories of their own. This is my odyssey, and it's one I have chosen to share with you, the reader.

I have chosen to share this with you because I know how it feels. I know what it's like to experience the juxtaposition of deep and abiding love for a child and not have that love reciprocated through easy, peaceful obedience. I have endured long, exhausting days of arguing, meltdowns and volatility. I have struggled to keep my composure and have wept with my son, Lee, as he purged the deepest wounds that have broken the family chain of a thousand generations.

And I have watched with great awe his ability to walk this earth with a piece of himself missing and still laugh and play. I have witnessed his perseverance in the face of obstacles that would have brought Atlas to his knees. I have felt his tender cheek slide across mine, warm as silk in the sun, and have had him melt into my arms while his eyes briefly found mine. We have seen the best in each other — and the worst.

I remember when an acquaintance stopped me in the grocery store. She told me about her son, then in upper elementary school, who had commented about Lee's coming home to us.

"Lee came all the way across the ocean by himself, mom. That was really brave," she told me he had said, her eyes filling with tears.

I had never thought about it that way. My son was brave. He *is* brave.

Telling this story is my way of being brave. I have not figured it all out, but I have spent a lot of time trying. I do not have all the answers, but I can tell you what worked for me. And I don't know the end of this narrative because I am writing to you from the trenches like an embattled soldier slowly discovering what it takes to stay strong. It is my opportunity to share what I have learned about finding peace and empowerment while parenting a child with challenging behaviors.

This is my mothering manifesto.

And I am writing it for you.

Introduction

Challenging behaviors come with the job of parenting, right? Every mom or dad can tell stories of temper tantrums and homework standoffs. Sometimes it even seems like a competition: who can top this? But there is a subset of parents who might not enter that competition, even though they have some doozies to share. These are the parents of children whose behaviors are just enough outside the box that they constantly doubt themselves, and their child.

If you believe and can relate to the idea that all kids struggle on some level, you're right, but this book is not written for you. This book is written for those of us whose parenting experiences are somewhere between typical and alarming. When it comes to parenting, "love and logic" is the standard I hear from most of my mom friends. My son has taught me that when your biological mother walks out of a room and never comes back, the world no longer seems loving or logical.

Lee just turned 13 years old. He is handsome, smart, intuitive, persistent and stubborn and loves to argue — with me. He is wildly observant and makes soulful inferences about the world more often than I know about because once in a while, he will make a comment that stops me in my tracks.

To the outside world he is a typical teenager. His room is a health hazard, his daily drive and motivation are highly self-selective, and his music preferences age me instantly. He rolls his eyes at my long dissertations on thinking positively and is sure I ask too much of him — like taking out the garbage or putting dishes from the counter into the dishwasher. But Lee isn't just like all the other kids in his 7th grade class. He came home to us in Wyoming at 19 months, after living with his birthmother and then a foster family in Korea. We were essentially his third family in less than two years.

In my previous life as a special education teacher I was familiar with the sad stories of some of our kids, but until Lee came along I didn't fully understand what those early experiences had done to them. Known as Adverse Childhood Experiences (ACES), certain early life events leave such an impression that they literally change developing neuropathways in the brain, creating a unique paradigm that is ultimately different from children who have not experienced them. For over a decade, the Center for Disease Control (CDC) has issued over 100 related articles on the ACE study. This study confirms that severe and chronic childhood trauma releases stress hormones that physically impact a child's developing brain. Such information was commensurate with what I have read about adopted children, the trauma of losing their primary caregiver and attachment disorders. For the purpose of this book, I will refer to this concept of stress's impact on a developing brain as attachment issues or early adverse experiences.

This knowledge informs how I parent, evaluate outside interventions, and collaborate with teachers within the school system. One of the chief ways that I advocate for my child is through educating others about the effects of early adverse experiences.

Our story is about adoption, but adverse childhood experiences come in many different flavors. One of the prime tasks of the first three years in life is forming a secure attachment to at least one primary caregiver. This task can be disrupted by illness (of the child or caregiver), unavoidable absences such as military deployment, death, abuse or neglect, and so on. Sometimes the origin is obvious and sometimes it's subtle. Adverse experiences can affect different children very differently. They often show up as some degree of attachment disorder and/or post-traumatic stress disorder. This book will not be a comprehensive treatise on ACES, but an account of my own journey as I learned what worked and didn't work for our family.

So you see, I have been *that* mom. The one the other mothers talked about (or at least I was sure they did). You are not alone, even though you might think you are. Many of us flounder behind closed doors without a way to adequately share our struggles. Often, we have no underlying proof of what is affecting our children. All we know is that the school calls us more frequently than our BFFs, the teachers are at a loss, and so are we. There appears to be no magic potion for conjuring behavioral bliss or creating lasting friendships for a child who tries too hard to make friends, but might not have them.

As parents, we pray our children are happy, well loved, successful and accepted. Our definitions of those things might vary, but ultimately it is probably safe to assume none of us wishes to watch our children struggle. In my case, I continue to seek a solution to Lee's Herculean academic efforts and my heartbreak when I observe the subtleties of his social insecurities. I constantly second-guess myself about what constitutes fair guidance versus what becomes enabling. Knowing when to advocate, when to protest, and when to step aside and give my son the gift of his own experience is an ebb and flow of gut feelings sprinkled with mindfulness and a keen awareness of my own hang-ups. It's not easy. I would tell you that I sometimes get it wrong, but I'm not so sure there are any right answers.

My intention for you, as you read this book, is that you will gain empowerment by claiming your inner adaptability and authority as you forge ahead with your own child who may be experiencing life just-outside-the-lines. My hope is that you will find resilience through personal reflection and inquiry, comfort for your suffering and an ease that you have not felt before when parenting and advocating for your child. I'll share my experience of being a special educator looking at the school system from the other side of the table, learning to navigate its limitations and fallibilities. And I'll use my training as a life coach to teach you how to care for yourself amidst the battle fatigue that is an inevitable part of parenting these kids.

I've spent many hours, days and years trying to "fix" my son in an attempt to make him more like his peers. But his early experiences have left an indelible stamp on him. He *is* different, but not worse. In many ways he is the better for what he went through. What if my child (and yours) doesn't need to be fixed, but just understood? What if the same is true for you and me, as parents? What if all we need is a shift in perspective and the confidence to go forth and get what we need?

So, pull up a chair. I invite you to share a cup of tea and some stories from the parental trenches with me. I've been where you are, and many others have too. I'm not a therapist, a doctor, a lawyer, or a scientist. I am a teacher. I am a mom. I am you.

Is your tea steeped now?

Good.

I'll start at the beginning...

LESSONS ON FINDING YOUR FOOTING

I believe one of the most sacrificial acts of love adoptive parents can do is to give up their preconceptions and agendas about what their child's views "should" be and be open to hear the conflicting emotions and thoughts their child often experiences.

Sherrie Eldridge

TWENTY THINGS ADOPTED KIDS WISH THEIR ADOPTIVE PARENTS KNEW

CHAPTER ONE

The Perfect Storm

For two long years, my husband and I tried to adopt a child. The initial process was both comical and discouraging. It required copious amounts of paperwork and we were subject to impromptu home visits that assured the powers that be that we were not harboring serial killers or dangerous exotic pets in our basement. The final interview was on parenting ideologies, and was conducted in public library study rooms in which my husband and I were separated and interrogated. It was akin to a cross-examination on *Locked Up Abroad*. How was I raised? How could my parents have improved their parenting styles? What kind of parenting strategies was I going to use on *our* child? Even with my special education degree and firm knowledge that theory doesn't always translate into practice, I was pretty sure I failed.

After months of scrutiny, we were deemed acceptable by our adoption counselor, the agency, the US government, and the state of Wyoming. You might think that kind of intensive perseverance would be rewarded, but alas, the wait for a child can be woefully long. For us, it was years.

We started with domestic adoption. We adhered to every pre-adoption step required and were assured that our file was being shared with those seeking adoptive parents. For months and months there was nothing. Maybe we just weren't that appealing.

As we waited, we were encouraged to explore alternate ideas like soliciting local doctors, lawyers and reproductive clinics. When dropping off our ridiculously glossy family brochures, I felt like we were advertising a cruise or elite summer camp rather than pursuing an adoption. But no matter our strategy, there was no response. The radio silence was deafening.

After months turned to years, we settled into life without the obsession overtaking us.

As sometimes happens, the change came on suddenly. That summer, I was recovering from a trifecta of misfortunes. All within a few months, a dear colleague had passed away from an aggressive form of brain cancer, my husband and I had survived a tornado while golfing, and the engine on my commercial plane failed when I was returning from a work conference. It was one of life's vortexes that leaves you weary and willing to give up control.

The morning after I finally arrived home from that ill-fated flight, I was nursing a cup of coffee and counting my blessings while I opened my accumulating email. One email in particular caught my eye. It was from our adoption agency.

I opened the letter to reveal the color photo of a 14-month-old boy from Korea sitting expressionless in his pink hanbok, a traditional form of Korean dress. He looked like an emperor, wise beyond his years. The agency wanted to know if we would like him for a son. Like a junior high love note, all you do is mark *Yes* or *No*.

In complete shock, we immediately wrote back: Yes! A million times, yes!

And then I panicked (or was that motherly instinct kicking in)? We had no idea when our son was coming, but we had a lot to do. In our case, nine months of preparation was a luxury we didn't have. We signed a forest's worth of forms, spent a small fortune on photocopies, passports and postage, and tracked down a notary public in a bar (she went to our church and was kind enough to meet us in a central location). The paperwork took weeks, although the coordinating agencies assured us they would do all they could to have our son home from Korea quickly.

It took three long months of updates and progress reports from the Korean agency before Lee came home. Then, without warning, the local agency called one evening to give us flight and pick up information. We would meet our *son* at Denver International Airport in three days. Three days! There is a lot you can do in three days, but I'm still not convinced preparing for a child is one of them.

It was November 2004 in northeastern Wyoming: cold, snowy, and hunting season. While I frantically called a friend to take me to the store to buy food, diapers, and clothing for our soon-arriving child, my husband dressed — and I don't mean in haute couture — an elk in our garage.

Reverting to his inner caveman seemed authentic to him in that moment, if completely insane to me.

Meanwhile, my hunting and gathering instincts were completely confounded by the ridiculous amount of sizes, textures and brands of everything toddler. I knew Lee was now 19 months old, but I had not stopped to convert his recently reported height and weight from the metric measurements Korea uses. I went by imagination, which completely summed up my parenting strategy right then. I also had to think about food. Did he drink milk, eat baby food or prefer fresh elk meat? I left the store frantic. I had not even thought to get a toy.

Adoption stories on television are inspirational and well-choreographed. You might think I, too, was overcome with delight and wonder like the families portrayed on the Hallmark channel. In truth, I was overwhelmed with fear. Would Lee scream at me, a stranger, when I took him from the airport? How would we explain this was our child as we wrestled him into our car? What if he hated me? I secretly wondered if buyer's remorse applied to the plane ticket purchased for my son.

Dave and I began our trip to the airport at 6:00 a.m. in a horrendous snowstorm that paralyzed our state. Our trek across the wide-open plains of Wyoming while listening to *In-Flight Korean* (I figured it would be helpful to know a few phrases) was painfully slow and treacherous. The *In-Flight Korean* CD mostly provided comic relief, because there was no way I could learn that language in an afternoon. By the time I had any use for Korean that day, I had learned to say, "Hello, my name is Mrs. Kim," which as we know is a lie. My name is *not* Mrs. Kim.

After more than six hours on the road, the snow-white meringue peaks of the airport appeared in the distance. There is video footage of us driving up to the airport, confirming the following conversation.

"There it is," Dave, my husband, whispered incredibly.

"Oh, my God," I said with stunned horror.

That is the extent of our dialogue. The footage consists mostly of me filming my husband's profile against endless bleak, snowy pastures. It's more of a silent film, a very tense silent film where you expect someone to jump out of the car.

We morphed into people who, even if for a brief moment, allowed an irrational thought to become a viable option.

"We could just not show up," I said out loud.

"They would probably find us."

"Would it be illegal if we just didn't go?" I honestly wondered.

We forcefully steered ourselves into the parking lot. I was chewing gum like a mad cow hoarding cud.

We emerged from the car as though we were doomed. It was a Hallmark moment, alright, but not the kind you see on TV.

"Have you ever been so scared in your life?"

"No," replied my husband. We weren't even speaking in hyperbole.

I was physically shaking. I just knew this poor little boy would recoil in terror at the well-intentioned white lady trying to take him out of the airport against his will. There would probably be equally well-meaning bystanders who would call the police to save the helpless little boy. My mind could no longer process what was happening. We solemnly marched our way to the arrival gate and waited while trying to stand upright. There were no banners, no family members, and no cheering. It's hard to convey the depth of isolation one can feel amid a throng of travelers.

The passengers disembarked in a sea of faces, first one wave, then another.

And then he emerged, dead asleep on the chaperone's shoulder.

Relief.

Awe.

Wonder.

Our journey of a million steps was beginning with this one amazing milestone.

With the agency director by our side now, we signed the papers in receipt of our amazing gift from Korea, a gesture so banal considering what had just happened. Mrs. Kim (that really was her name) took the completed papers and wished us well. That was it. She oversaw the exchange and walked away. I took Lee in my arms, lugged him to the waiting car, strapped him into his car seat and sat beside him in the back seat. As he woke up, I fed him his bottle and mimicked his Korean intonations. He locked eyes with me and smiled. At least he had not screamed bloody murder in the airport.

The trip home was harrowing in the nighttime snow that continued to batter the Denver area that day. We resigned ourselves to spending our first night together in a hotel room, despite our fear of disrupting nearby patrons once this cute little boy figured out the depth of what had just transpired in his life.

Thankfully, his travel pack had familiar toys and snacks that would help to keep him occupied most of the night. I ingratiated myself to him by offering him a warm bath (in Korean) and plenty of snacks. He delighted in the water and played for a long time while I vigilantly watched his every move and started breathing again. I pulled out the pajamas I had purchased, but they were too small. My husband handily cut out the feet with a Swiss Army knife he kept in the car. Everything felt so awkward.

Lee was soothed by bottles of milk and snacks, which we happily provided at every hint of discomfort — physical or emotional. We did this into the wee hours of the morning until he threw up on himself, me and the hotel linens. After that, he fell into a peaceful slumber on my chest.

That was his entry into our world. We arrived at our house the next day. He recovered from jet lag rather quickly, and we set out to establish routines and get to know one another.

Settling in

When my husband finally returned to work, Lee and I looked at each other, wondering what in the world we were supposed to do now. Lee tried in vain to befriend our curmudgeonly cat, while I tried to befriend Lee, with slightly greater success. Lee became my sidekick, my buddy, following me every waking moment and doing whatever I did. It was a time of personal exploration and bonding, much like figuring out complicated steps to a choreographed dance you join halfway through the song. Missteps were plentiful, but we held on and kept going.

In retrospect, we were all in survival mode when Lee came home. We did all the typical day-to-day things — grocery shopping, going to the park, attending church on Sundays — but every attempt to invoke "normalcy" was quietly shrouded in the seismic shift that had resulted in our new life together.

For that first year, we continued to find our footing. Every day, that little guy was my hero. At the age of 19 months, he had flown across the ocean and was bravely making the most of a foreign country with foreign parents who did not speak his language. He was a sponge, learning sign language (recommended to facilitate communication) and English simultaneously. He assimilated quickly — and maybe even a little sadly — as his deep Korean bows of respect gave way to spoken words of thanks and his soft, quiet voice found a crescendo to match the volume of his peers (when he arrived, even his loud voice could not be heard from room to room).

We attended a local mother's group, had playdates and spent hours at the park and pool. He loved music, playing with friends, and snuggling in for a bedtime story with me. We read the same books so many times that he could recite them. He was happy, curious and game for almost anything. In an attempt to be the perfect mom, I filled up our calendar like a maniac. I'm not sure what I was trying to keep up with or outrun, but we definitely kept a dizzying pace. Maybe I was afraid that if we stopped long enough, we would feel the full emotional impact of what the hell had just happened.

About six months into my new role as doting mother, something notable happened. Lee and I were downstairs playing on a slide (a gift from co-workers) when he let out a relaxed, hearty giggle. I distinctly remember that exact moment because I knew we had experienced a breakthrough. After six months, Lee was finally relaxed enough to actually *laugh*. The shroud gently protecting his personality from us, strangers, had been lifted. It was like opening the curtains on a sunny day. His face, his feelings, everything about him was clearer and more animated. If you did not know our circumstances, you would have never known this subtle, yet telling, shift in Lee's disposition.

And then everything started getting real. Very real.

Making Connections

There was an indescribable intensity to our life that was hard to communicate to my mom friends. When I shared stories about being in the trenches of toddlerhood, as we do, my mom friends were sympathetic and understanding, but only to the point they could relate. Lee and I were the same as every other mother-son set, yet the intensity of our daily existence, imperceptible to others in the words I shared, was something a little north of normal. The creeping fingers of fatigue and frayed nerves deepened my longing for connection and, at times, challenged my coping skills.

Lee's fear of being alone and the residual heartbreak of having already twice lost his primary caregivers bubbled to the surface, threatening our family's equilibrium. His shrieks when I left the room or when he felt frustrated penetrated every cell in my body. When I heard that harrowing screech, there was no mistaking his disapproval. It made me want to shove a knitting needle into my ear. My cousin experienced it when she came for a brief stay from Australia. Years later, when she had her own child who shrieked for long stints as an infant, she admitted that, until then, she had never fully grasped the wearing toll of such a sound.

Lee's cries did not abate at night. I remember once, after a particularly rough patch at Christmas the year after Lee came home, I finally confessed to a friend that Lee was having night terrors. They were heartbreaking to hear in the dark of night. His bereft screams shook his entire body and nothing could be done to console him. Each time a night terror came, it was easy to imagine that he was reliving the moment when his birthmother had walked out the door after surrendering him to the adoption agency at 14 months, never to return. His cheeks would be soaked with tears and in those moments between unconscious and conscious, his despair was tangible. I often cried myself, helpless to comfort my baby. His pain was palpable.

Night terrors are common for internationally adopted children. Nightmares are also common among children who aren't adopted, so other moms were quick to commiserate with me. But, somewhere deep inside, their efforts to connect left me unsatisfied, mostly because I attached so much heartache to our intermittent night episodes that I told myself only someone with a similar experience could truly understand the terror that shattered our nights.

My desperation to understand and connect with my growing son rippled out into relationships with other moms. The comparisons I made between us whispered that I was not good enough. Lee and I were obviously swimming upstream while everyone else had found the current. But the whispers could be quelled if we were busy and engaged on playdates and field trips designed to let the kids play and the moms visit.

I met a great friend at our mother's group and we quickly became inseparable. We laughed that she was a playground stalker because she followed us home from the group one day and introduced herself, but I was so glad. Most of my friends had been colleagues. They still worked every day while I suited up in shiny new yoga pants and a practical ponytail. After spending time together in the park, I was elated to have found Ellen. She was thoughtful, supportive and we had a lot in common. We hung out often and our kids played splendidly together. Our families enjoyed dinners together and we swapped date nights so that one couple could go out while the other would host the dating couple's child. It was such a great match, and it was my first important relationship with another at-home mom.

Ellen had a sweet way about her. She was friendly with everyone and often gathered friends for holidays and baking extravaganzas. She was the quintessential hostess and I can't emphasize enough her kindness and compassion. Did I mention she would show up with steaming hot Starbucks on a Sunday morning because she *felt like it*? She was better than a husband! But all that perfection had a downside for me that I was never to forget.

The first time I felt the public inadequacy of my parenting started out as a day like any other. Our children were playing while Ellen and I sat and enjoyed a cup of tea in her sunny living room. Her taste was impeccable, from her clothes to her home. That day we talked about wildly important things like pedicures, film plots and craft ideas (which I love about as much as the idea of a lobotomy).

The incident was innocuous, but my interpretation was impactful. Basically, I said something to my child out loud. I meant what I said as a correction, but, at some point, Ellen stepped in and took over the conversation. I only remember her coming back to the couch afterwards, settling in with her tea and telling me that I didn't need to be so hard on Lee. I probably nodded and sipped my tea while the moment seared itself into my mind for all eternity like a red hot iron on leather.

Honestly, Ellen was only trying to help. She felt comfortable enough to help discipline (or protect?) my child and was confident enough in that moment to take the lead. I was probably parenting inertly from the couch while she was willing to put her tea down and get up to optimize a teachable moment. Perhaps guilt over my secret desire to lounge around with a warm cup and a deep need for a parenting vacation while she leapt into the foray got the best of me.

As our friendship blossomed, my secret home life simmered below the surface. Quiet time with Lee was spent playing, baking and reading together. We took walks, explored the outdoors and made it to the gym, where he was warming up to the idea of playing with other kids while I got some much-needed exercise. Our routine was becoming comfortable, predictable.

After naps, Lee would wake up emotionally dysregulated and grouchy, which is typical for children affected by attachment issues. Any attempt to shift his mood was met with loud resistance. His predictable late afternoon protests were usually about things like wearing socks, snack selections and the sun shining the wrong way. The whining could last for hours. Dinnertime felt futile and unpleasant as he writhed around demanding my full attention. I knew of other toddlers who lost resolve around dinnertime, but our daily ritual of discontent seemed like the extended version of a techno song whose pulsating beat goes on long after the melody is over. My husband, who worked exhaustive hours, usually found me ready to be tapped out of the day-long wrestling match.

When a fellow special education teacher came to visit, we were lucky that she observed this dinnertime behavior. Lee was in rare form. You have to give the kid kudos for his absolute persistence. I mean, even now, his stamina and determination are admirable. Unfazed, my friend suggested that we try behavior modification. Behavior modification, used often by teachers, is the attempt to eliminate undesirable behaviors by using positive reinforcement. Call it what you will, it works well on children, carrier pigeons and dolphins at Sea World.

We sat there for what seemed like an eternity as Lee carried on. As soon as he would breathe, it would go quiet for a moment, so she would praise him. And he would begin again with the wailing and gnashing of teeth. He was particularly unhappy with her intrusion on the undivided attention he thought I should be giving him. We both tried to keep up the behavior modification charade, but it is exhausting (especially when you aren't being paid) and we didn't get much visiting done. As I recall, she wished me luck and told me to keep it up until the behavior was extinguished. She ran to her truck and headed back to the country, where the only sounds of discontent were lowing cattle and chirping crickets.

Bedtime was an entirely different operation. We started with a soothing bath, which Lee loved. It was a nice time to reconnect from the day and watch him laugh. Transitioning out of the tub to his bed was definitely more about containment, but Dave and I were getting to be pros and could wrangle Lee into bed with the promise of many stories and someone staying until he fell asleep. His bedtime routine, even into elementary school, took up to two hours. It was a time of cuddles, relaxation and connection. It was also time-consuming.

At night, Lee still slept with us, despite our desperate efforts to transition him into his own bed. As he grew older and more restless, our king-sized bed resembled a full-contact interpretation of one of the *Five Little Monkeys* stories — only there were three of us, two of whom required full-body armor and protective helmets. Needless to say, we were all tired.

I'm sure some parents would think we were crazy to indulge our child like that. I have heard many times that we should have just put him to bed and let him cry it out. We tried. My mom, while visiting for Christmas one year, was of the same opinion. A veteran of five children, my mom lasted less than thirty seconds after she put Lee in his bed and shut the door. There was something in his cry that was just too profound and poignant to ignore. Many parents had great advice, although it seemed few of them were trying to survive the many battles I was as I teetered precariously between satisfying the deep-seated needs of a wary child and caving in to the manipulative demands of an over-indulged one. I have chosen the former more than I have the latter; not that it has made me right.

Our child, even years after his arrival into our loving home, was still wary of trust and security. It was hard to determine how much love and indulgence was too much. When a typically parented infant cries, his needs are met over and over again. This creates a pattern of safety and trust. In Lee's case, that pattern had been established, too, but it had been disrupted — twice. First, he had to leave his birth family, and then he had to leave his foster family. The established behavior our son knew was that people will take care of you and then dump you off with new people to start over. We had to start our relationship off as though he were an infant so that he could trust and believe that his needs would be met with us. At least, we bought into that theory. Unfortunately, to some parents, it looked and sounded like indulgence and enabling.

Maybe it was indulgent, but according to everything I had read, internationally adopted children can lag behind their peers socially and academically by as many months as they are old when they come home. If that was true, then Lee had the potential to be nearly two years behind his peers emotionally, which would explain his need for a lengthy bedtime ritual, a constant need for attention and a fear of being alone that was inconsistent with kids his own age. It has also been documented that, although life after adoption could bring about many opportunities, it was apparent that the influence of the past did not completely disappear.

Fear of being alone contributed to fatigue and dysregulation for both Lee and me. Not knowing this was a symptom of insecure attachment, I listened to Lee talk non-stop. I was delighted at his easy language acquisition, but I realized I was doing absolutely everything with endless background noise and a constant demand for my engagement. This behavior created a heightened awareness in me, occasionally leading to irritability and an understandable longing for life in a monastery. A vow of silence seemed golden.

Constant chatter is typical for toddlers, but, again, the intensity was relentless. My child would not put together a puzzle without me sitting right next to him, nor would I ever find him in his room alone as a toddler. Ever. The first day I found him in his room by himself, he was in elementary school and it was momentous. And it lasted three minutes.

Tantrums, a hallmark of toddlerhood, were just as present in our home as everyone else's. Unlike other children,

Lee would occasionally blow past the typical three-year-old fit protocol to a deeper, more pained emotional state like nothing I have encountered in a child. The depth of his release would grip his entire body. His wailing would become primal, like the noise of night terrors in the conscious light of day. There was no parental reasoning or comfort that could quell that kind of suffering in a child. He would also lash out, which prompted me to feel even more isolated. As he grew, we were inching towards something ever more north of normal.

I didn't know anyone else who was having a similar parenting experience. Occasionally, I tried to express my fears and frustrations, but the stories I shared fell short of the truth or were told with humor, as though I had it under control. I would blind people with my dazzling (or convoluted) attachment-speak and try to normalize everything. I worked hard to keep the façade intact, but a feeling of isolation and despair was encroaching upon me.

I remember going through a particularly grueling parenting patch with little sleep or down time for me. If I had been an electronic device, my battery charge would have been below 50%. What Lee required from me as his mom didn't always pair well with my need for sleep and personal space.

One afternoon, Ellen and her daughter came over. Being together with Ellen and her daughter was a near-daily experience. On this particular day, the kids played while Ellen and I merrily made ourselves a gourmet lunch of wraps with fancy greens, just like those offered in quaint, upscale cafes. I don't remember the exact moment of impact, but Lee pushed my buttons enough that I walked him forcefully down the hall, picked him up and set him down in his room, door wide open. I returned to our lunch. However, my "meltdown" filled the air with an awkwardness that laid bare my secret guilt and shame. For me, it underscored my shortcomings and failure to remain eternally composed in the face of a child who needed me to be in control at all times as proof that he could trust me and that I could keep him safe. If the truth were known, I failed over and over again. This time, I had failed out loud, in front of my friend.

Here's the moment I remember most: I wrote Ellen an apology note afterward. In it, I told her that I was sorry for losing my temper and sincerely apologized that she had to witness my lack of composure, and how embarrassing it was for me to have done that in front of her. I mailed it. That was that. Hopefully, we would move forward and I would get a better grip on my emotions.

Happily, the incident did not overtly affect our relationship or temper our get-togethers. The next time we got together though, she mentioned receiving my card and thanked me for the apology. What I didn't anticipate was how that apology exchange made me feel.

Ellen was probably relieved that I wasn't a regular child-abuser, and I was glad she was willing to let bygones be bygones. But her specific acceptance of my apology translated into an unequivocal validation of what I viewed as my own huge inadequacies. In a passive way, I had been reaching out with that card. What I was really saying was: *I'm sorry I lost my cool. This is hard and I need help*! But hey, I can't blame the woman for not being able to read my mind. That's a tough skill to master.

For a while, I protected my ego around other moms whose children were seemingly "perfect." I was swimming too hard up stream to appreciate their buoyancy in the tide pool of parenting. Instead, I backed away from relationships that validated my greatest fears about motherhood, and sought out friends that felt safe. I needed women who were all about imperfection, who found Lee's escapades endearing and could see the humor in some of it. I did *not* need judgment and condemnation, however politely or tacitly expressed.

To my delight, I eventually found a group of friends who were good at mind reading and with whom I could comfortably tell my tales. I knew they were going to be my saving grace after I walked in for a lunch gathering and told them about Lee berating a Catholic nun after preschool pick-up earlier that day. The poor, godly woman, close to returning to the mother house for retirement, tried to talk to Lee in a sweet voice, asking how he had liked school that morning. He told her to shut up and started screaming. It's impossible to excuse yourself from a moment like that with any decorum or dignity. I almost died! Who yells at a nun?! I'll tell you who: my son at the age of four, God bless him.

As I told the ladies my story, I started to cry. It was one of those moments where cumulative helplessness and effortful struggle converge, creating a much-needed physical release. I was embarrassed to be crying over what seemed like a trivial matter, but they just laughed at the prospect of a four-year-old chewing out a nun and empathized over the mortification of it all.

"Our group isn't just a friendship, it's a ministry," said one of them as she hugged me.

And thank goodness.

Even though I felt like no one could fully comprehend the scope of my parenting challenges, I would lean on these ladies for a very long time. And it didn't hurt a bit that they liked good food, tea, desserts and laughter as much as I did.

Emerging Theories & Symptoms of Attachment Disorder

Along with friends, books and the Internet became my steady parenting companions. I pieced together theories about attachment, post-traumatic stress, and the neurological development of children with adverse childhood experiences (ACEs). I slowly started to share what I learned as a means of processing my own experience and helping others in similar circumstances.

Reactive Attachment Disorder (RAD), a term I hesitate to use in our situation because of its egregious implications, has historically been presented as a terrible affliction with a bleak future for adopted and mistreated children. I have seen several sensational network exposés on children adopted from orphanages who are highly volatile and potentially homicidal towards their adoptive families. Those exposés established what RAD looked like to me. The situations portrayed on TV seemed hopeless and despairing.

After a decade of raising Lee, I continue to learn about emerging theories on children with ACEs and RAD. Both of these acronyms, like many others that label groups of behaviors for the purposes of treating and fixing, have a range of intensities. Ours happens to be on the manageable side of mild. Many kids like Lee are just like their peers, with a subtle set of behaviors you may not notice if you don't know them well. Lee appears to be a typical kid in almost every circumstance, but there are social and emotional behaviors derived from his early experiences that can create challenges for him.

We have always heard from teachers and other adults that Lee is polite, hardworking and has lots of friends. From my perspective, he struggles to form intimate friendships, has difficulty with homework and continues to assimilate his racial differences and his past. However, despite his background there is no doubt he is one of the most persistent, resilient, intuitive, kind, and clever kids I know.

If you are interested in learning more about the symptoms of attachment disorders or the formal identifying factors of adverse childhood experiences, I would invite you to read results from the CDC study mentioned earlier, or watch the TED talk by Nadine Burke Harris on how early trauma affects health across a lifetime. It explains a lot about the correlations we are learning between early trauma and brain development. While she has found a correlation within the medical field, I would argue that there are implications for schools and parents, too.

Nancy Thomas, of Families By Design, is a successful therapeutic foster parent and speaker who has written several books on the topic of early trauma, parenting and attachment disorders. Thomas, having experienced early trauma herself, speaks candidly about her experiences and observations while parenting very difficult children. Her methods and philosophies are a mix of brain research, "Love and Logic" and animal training. Many of the symptoms and causes she lists that are associated with attachment disorder have proven helpful for us and may be helpful for all children who have had adverse childhood experiences that have disrupted their attachment during formative years. Keep in mind that these symptoms range from mild to extreme!

Attachment Disorder Symptoms

- Superficially engaging and charming

- Lack of eye contact on parents' terms

- Indiscriminately affectionate with strangers

- Not affectionate on parents' terms (not "cuddly")

- Destructive to self, others and material things ("accident prone")

- Cruelty to animals

- Lying about the obvious ("crazy" lying)

- Stealing

- No impulse controls (frequently acts hyperactive)

- Learning lags

- Lack of cause-and-effect thinking

- Lack of conscience

- Abnormal eating patterns

- Poor peer relationships

- Preoccupation with fire

- Preoccupation with blood and gore

- Persistent nonsense questions and chatter

- Inappropriately demanding and clingy

- Abnormal speech patterns

Taken From: *Thomas, N. (Families by Design) (2008, February 7). "Children with Reactive Attachment Disorder." Lecture conducted from Parent Information Center in Buffalo, Wyoming.*

Causes

Any of the following conditions occurring to a child during the first 36 months of life puts them at risk for attachment disorder, or attachment behaviors associated with Adverse Childhood Experiences:

- Unwanted pregnancy

- Pre-birth exposure to trauma, drugs or alcohol

- Abuse (physical, emotional, sexual)

- Neglect (not answering the baby's cries for help)

- Separation from primary caregiver (e.g., due to illness or death of mother, or severe illness or hospitalization of the baby, or adoption)

- On-going pain such as colic, hernia or many ear infections

- Changing day cares or using providers who don't do bonding

- Having a mom with chronic depression

- Going through several moves or placements (foster care, failed adoptions)

- Being a baby cared for on a timed schedule or other self-centered parenting technique

It is my opinion that the more we continue to learn about the impact of ACEs on the brain and behavior, the better we can help children and adults heal with appropriate support and interventions.

According to Thomas, N. (Families by Design) (2008, February 7). "Children with Reactive Attachment Disorder." Lecture conducted from Parent Information Center in Buffalo, Wyoming.

Because of his early childhood experiences, Lee exhibits behaviors commonly seen in children with attachment disorders. It's important to note that he has never been medically diagnosed because we have had no need to pursue a label. That's what makes parenting some children so unique and difficult. These children seem so typical or just this side of "naughty" that adults may not even consider that their reactions and behaviors are based on core beliefs formed during early severe and chronic stress. It is my belief that Lee's brain operates on the premise that families are not permanent, and that in the end everyone leaves. That must be a sad and panicky feeling. Often, his core beliefs have created reactions based on what he thought was true, and those reactions resulted in behaviors that seemingly reinforced his initial beliefs, producing a negative spiral. Those behaviors became even more curious and concerning when he headed off to school.

CHAPTER TWO

The Antithesis of Academic Achievement

Lee greeted me every day after school by throwing his backpack at me full force, as if to physically unburden himself of the day's restraint imposed by a regimented, rule-laden environment. His aggressive gesture, unnoticed by most everyone, spoke volumes to me. I became the receptacle into which he poured his frustrations, anger and disappointment. He would emerge from the school doors, run down a slight hill and launch his backpack like the star of an after school special on using school paraphernalia as weapons. I resented the backpack flying at me every day. I also had no idea how to make it stop.

Before long, I unconsciously put on my parenting armor before picking him up. As the clock crept towards afternoon pick-up, I felt anxious butterflies in my stomach and a mental resistance to the evening ahead. Unknowingly, I was building my own neuropathways based on chronic stress from my current experiences.

Like many full-time kindergarten children, Lee grew fatigued as the week progressed. Inevitably, I could count on a release of big feelings and overwhelm on Thursday evenings. Most kids do this at least occasionally, but ours sometimes turned it into the extended version — the one where a typical melt down subtly shifted to something far deeper than weariness from school. It was weariness of life, a reaction to an emotional wound that could not be fixed with an after school hug or a cookie.

The outbursts became more and more frequent with the addition of school. Requiring Lee to be "on" all day took so much of his energy. He had so little left for coping at the end of the day that it only made a release more prevalent, sustained and necessary. He could now carry on intensely for hours, triggered seemingly by the most trivial of matters. All I did was try to hold him as he did everything to keep me away.

Adding typical school activities like soccer or baseball made our evenings as unpredictable as walking through a field of unmarked land mines. Soccer required long, tight socks that sent him into convulsions because they would never go on right. When I tied his shoes, they were often too tight or too loose. Team jerseys were itchy or the wrong color. Getting him dressed and ready for sports, a pastime he excelled at and enjoyed, could literally take hours. Sensory sensitivities and a low frustration tolerance are classic signs of attachment issues and contributed to our daily struggles. Football was the worst. The numerous straps, buttons, pads and an ill-fitting helmet almost sent me to an asylum. It didn't help that the coach, citing upfront that he wasn't interested in any parental input, basically ignored Lee's initial pleas that his helmet was too tight and uncomfortable. He relented only when I confessed that my son was playing with a wad of medical gauze I had shoved up into the nooks and crannies of the cranium-squeezing headgear.

There were many times I lost my cool trying to get us to practices or games. I was a Type A mom with an agenda and dwindling empathy for an emotionally dysregulated boy expressively telling me why long, tight socks were driving him crazy. I figured if we could just suit him up and get through the activity, we could move through his big feelings later. Like opposing magnetic poles, I was hindering more than helping. With every ounce of resistance he showed, I could match him. The entire exercise became explosive for both of us.

I never let the coaches in on our pre-game rituals, so being on time caused a lot of stress. There were a handful of times that we skipped practice when he was very young and imperfect attendance was not detrimental to his participation. As he grew older, though, teams and coaches required regular attendance at practice and games. And the coaches didn't want excuses. Sometimes, I wish I could have explained what the hour preceding practice had been like at our house, but most coaches, seemingly uninterested in anything other than the bootstrap theory, were mostly about sucking it up and keeping on.

The kids on Lee's teams and in school also started to become Lee's friends. Lee has always been a friendly, forgiving child who happily played with anyone. I have always been so impressed with his ability to befriend anyone. When he was invited to other people's houses, I unfailingly received a glowing report about his good manners and pleasant disposition.

But when friends came to our house, I went into overdrive. Lee exhibited controlling behaviors that left his guests exasperated at always having to go last, endure impromptu rule changes to games (the odds were ever in Lee's favor) and having to use the lesser-quality toys. Lee cleverly convinced them to do what he wanted, and often dismissed his guest's requests and desires.

I put a lot of pressure on myself when we had Lee's friends over. I became hyper-vigilant to the territorial behavior that seemed to possess him on his home turf. The reciprocity of hosting kids seemed so easy for other moms, while hosting play dates became a major ordeal for me. Sleepovers were especially difficult, and they still are. Despite my best efforts to show him how it feels to be last or not have an equal number of turns, his need to control an environment appears unconscious and overwhelming; something akin to animalistic survival.

Even now, he has a revolving door of friends. He has hosted many buddies for sleepovers, but very few return for an encore. I have not been able to determine if it's because Lee moves along to another friend quickly, or if the other child becomes ambivalent. My husband and I can truly become heartbroken over Lee's lack of ability to bond with other kids his age. He tries so hard to fit in. And yet, his effervescence and enthusiasm about teammates and school chums is astounding to me. He never seems down about being at home when he knows others are out having fun. I'm just never sure if his feelings are bottled up somewhere or if his ability to compartmentalize emotional baggage is so sophisticated that he simply packs it away faster than I can pack away carbohydrates at an Italian buffet. After all, he is the master of emotionally shutting down.

Just like when he arrived as a toddler, shutting down is as easy for Lee as breathing. It's another way of securing his survival and safety.

Many times I have tried to crack his feeling state. It's not often that confessions of being teased or overwhelmed with schoolwork make it into even the most loving and supportive conversations. Whenever I seem to be making progress on getting him to reveal his true feelings, his redirection is like a conversational torpedo sinking my hopes of gaining access to his internal life. It must feel so isolated in his world. Based on his behavior, I know he is hurting, but finding the language to express his feelings has always eluded him. I know that can be true for most children, but there is something keenly real about Lee's ability to test relationships and to shut down faster than a lemonade stand in a thunderstorm. And when he shuts down, it can challenge the emotional mettle of even well-meaning professionals not to reciprocate in kind.

The best example of this was in fifth grade. He had worked for three hard years in a very supportive school environment and the principal, also his part-time teacher for two years, took special interest in making sure Lee was successful. She was not only effective in helping him academically, but she talked to him in quiet moments and did everything she could to empower him to become his own advocate. She is one teacher that I know poured her heart and soul into Lee. She attended his violin concerts, came to a few baseball games and invited him over to her house. I would be lying if I told you she did this only for Lee, because the woman was an amazing testament to teachers. She really loved her students and treated them like a mother would. She corrected them firmly when necessary, but did everything she could to encourage and support them.

In fourth grade, during the end-of-year ceremony in which teachers recited special anecdotes about the students that year, she could not tell of Lee's immense strides and growth in confidence without crying. You could tell they had both worked hard through the year and had formed a special bond. She often told me how much he had warmed up to her, trusted her and could look her in the eye when they spoke. She beamed. So did Lee.

"You know, I think I actually heard him really *laugh* this year!" she once said to me.

I knew exactly what she meant. It was a redux of that day in the basement with me. He had finally let her "see" him. The real him.

The next year, she moved up with Lee's class. The loving kindness she held for Lee continued. I was in awe of her dedication to him and was so thankful for every ounce of it. If Lee hit a bump, we would confer immediately. She was open to suggestions, wanted to know what I knew and often came up with spectacular ideas of her own that usually worked wonders. She could read him like I could.

By the spring of his fifth grade year, I believe he started to test her. She called a few times to tell me that he was shutting down, not doing his work, off task. Nothing she did evoked productivity. I empathized and reminded her that this had happened every spring. It was like clockwork, a pattern. Whether it was fatigue or a mental "I'm done," he really did have a hard time sprinting to the finish. I saw the apathy at home too. It frustrated me equally.

She eventually confessed, "There isn't anything I can do. He just doesn't want to do anything for me."

If there was anything I knew, it was how exhausting seemingly lazy behaviors could be. I knew they were a test of resolve, not for Lee, but for the adult. He needed to know that you could stick with it, hang with him, even when he couldn't hang with himself.

In my estimation, his retreat made her feel defeated. She had emptied herself into this kid who had thrived under her tutelage for years. As the year dwindled and her magic dissipated, she seemed hurt. I knew it was never personal and I'll never know what happened exactly, but I felt something had changed.

In the final weeks of school, she appeared less engaged with Lee and had no more desire to counter his ambivalence. The end-of-year ceremony saw her struggling to say anything of substance. She said that he was well-behaved and good at gym. She was stoic, almost robotic, clearly tempering the disappointment that had created the riff just weeks before school let out. During the ceremony, Lee was devoid of emotion, too. He looked ahead and stiffened at having to stand near her as she read her scripted anecdotes. His eyes were empty. I knew that look, too. He was over and out.

I noticed he had not received the Presidential Award for Physical Education that year either. After school was out, I worked up the nerve to ask about it. She responded in a text:

Lee did not dress out for PE two weeks in a row. As a result, he will not be receiving the award. Those are the rules.

I was conflicted. I completely understood that he had violated the PE rules, and yet that was one of the only activities I have ever seen him actually try to achieve in, by keeping his scores on a bedroom blackboard and constantly deducting how many sit-ups, chin-ups and other tasks he would have to do to earn the Presidential ranking.

I called a dear friend and former teacher who acknowledged that I was waffling. "Too bad he knew he needed to dress out and he didn't. That's a bummer."

I asked Lee, "Did you miss not being given the Presidential Award?"

"No."

"Why didn't you dress out for PE?" I was curious.

"Because it takes too long and I can do PE in my uniform."

Knowing that he had met all the criteria to receive the award seemed to be enough for Lee. But the entire episode made me sad. The teacher never told me that he was not dressing out for PE. She had stopped our communication. Her sudden, aloof demeanor hurt me, although Lee never indicated that anything was amiss in his world. He was simply glad for summer.

Perhaps he was used to this feeling of being abandoned, given up on. He'd known it was coming the whole time. His friends, his teachers and even his two previous families had left him. According to his experience, nobody stuck around, especially once they knew you. There were plenty of kids for a teacher to love, why stick with him? This self-perpetuating belief informed his behaviors, his words and the ever-growing wall around his heart. Months later, I would relay this story to Eureka, my counselor. It still hung over me like the stench of a 12-year-old boy's gym shoes.

She validated what I knew, that the teacher had understandably followed the rules, but Eureka also validated that when we deal with kids who have attachment issues, the preservation of a relationship cannot be underestimated. These kids will make relationships tough on purpose, to see how long adults or peers will last. While most parents and schools embrace natural consequences and the principles of "love and logic," both equally effective strategies, you can imagine how a child who has experienced neglect, abuse or the loss of a primary caregiver might not see the world as loving or logical. Therefore, punitive consequences, emotional withdrawal or the withholding of an award can validate a deep-seated, fundamental belief that they are not worth it.

And this is where it gets tricky. This is where, as parents with this type of child, we understand the divergence of our path from the one most parents and teachers walk. We begin to walk the road less traveled. We intuitively recognize that our child might be able to "suck it up" when issued natural consequences, but that little learning is imparted (or at least not the learning that we want them to have). What we know is that our child's impaired neurology may require a more gentle and relationship-oriented solution to what may seem like typical developmental problems, but are really emotional barometers intended to gauge the validity of their impaired core beliefs.

Between school and activities, Lee was absolutely laid bare every day from all that was required of him. Like a grain of sand in a shoe, the struggle to hold all of us together at home wore on me. I think that's the nature of living with a child with adverse childhood experiences. It takes a lot of effort and stamina to hold all the big feelings that leak out while consistently reinforcing appropriate ways to deal with their emotions and frustrations.

While home was hard, being in public had its own challenges. When Lee was younger and I taught Zumba, for instance, a Latin dance-based fitness class, he would sneak out of the daycare room, run up behind me and smack me on the butt in front of my participants, who usually laughed. He craftily planned sneak attacks at school too, which eventually kept me from volunteering and participating in school activities. Most every stay-at-home mom I knew joined the school's parent group and volunteered in the classroom. Being near my child in public required lots of personal resolve and a witty retort to dismiss and excuse his missiles of shock and awe.

When Lee was in kindergarten, I volunteered to read to the class once a week. I confirmed then that Lee had difficulty with me being at school. He jockeyed to be right beside me and tried to dominate any group I read to. When I listened to individuals read in the classroom, Lee insisted I only read with him. He was beside himself if anyone else edged him out, which happened a few times. His behavior was so radically different that I often heard things like, "Wow, I have never seen that from him before," from teachers. It was one of the great secrets we kept. The way he treated me was not commensurate with the way he treated most other people — including his dad. He would glare at me, pinch me clandestinely, or whisper inappropriate things at odd times. He tested me and my love more than he did with any other relationship, seemingly daring me to leave him as his other mothers had.

Being at school with Lee had taken so much energy that once the year was over, I was out of the class-volunteering business. I showed up for special occasions like Thanksgiving and Christmas programs, having geared myself up for the inevitable onset of wild, inexplicable and potentially embarrassing behavior.

Most children were excited to have their parents come for special days. The moms were usually dressed fashionably, hair done... and while I did the same, I also had to cloak myself in the usual parenting armor necessary for whatever secret arrow my child would sling during the program. School was definitely making our lives a little more complicated. I could barely manage my own feelings, let alone his. And that didn't even cover the academic concerns that started piling on top of the nuclear emotions that were emerging.

The Academic Conundrum

The beginning of first grade harbored foreboding. Within the first week, Lee was caught "cheating" on a spelling test. He had never seen a spelling test before, but the pressure to perform had gotten the better of him. The teacher called to explain what had happened and that Lee was headed to detention. I was mortified. I secretly wondered if Lee was headed for a life of crime (I may have overreacted). He came home visibly upset and we had a few particularly bad days. As the weeks slipped by, I noticed that he had swiped someone's lunch card and then small, single paint palettes from the art room appeared. Each time I discovered odd items in his backpack, which I searched regularly now, my stomach churned. I notified respective teachers about the "thefts."

His classroom teacher, after consulting with me, talked with Lee and made a big deal about stealing, telling him that next time he would have to serve more detention. Our sidebar collaboration helped me feel supported and hopeful. The art teacher, acting independently, took her own approach to the paint theft. She called Lee to her classroom via loud-speaker and confronted him. The paint was returned and I convinced myself that Lee deserved her wrath. Maybe it would scare him straight.

Since Lee turned over his backpack each day with bodily force, it was easy for me to search it. I dreaded those back-pack scans, because whenever I found something I would spiral into crime scenarios ripped from the headlines. It was dreadful. My poisoned thinking paralyzed my good sense and I failed to recognize my own triggers. All I felt was fear and failure. What would people think about us? What did the teachers think about Lee?

The entire stealing episode had been the result of a spell-ing test gone wrong. He had not had one before, he knew he had to perform and he used whatever means were neces-sary to hide his own known deficits. When I wasn't walking around singing the theme song to *Cops*, I was debating whether or not his lag in academics was a result of anxiety and hyper-vigilance or a legitimate learning disability. The dichotomy introduced yet another parenting paradox.

When Lee was in preschool, he omitted the number six when he counted. I also remember typical letter reversals and the letter sounds that were right one day and wrong the next. He had never made up his own spontaneous picture-book story and resisted putting together story sequencing cards. He hated sit-down reading activities, although he always loved when I read to him. In an attempt to keep him up on academics (and as a secret way of informally assessing his skills) I employed an armada of programs like Hooked on Phonics, computer reading games, auditory recognition programs, and research-based Direct Instruction programs that were scripted and structured for in-depth reading remediation. Because I had worked in special education with students with learning disabilities, I knew where to find all of the resources I needed to become my child's supplemental teacher.

I thought I was helping, what with my degree and experience in the classroom. Surely he would understand that just working a little harder at home would make his school day a little easier and the test scores a little higher. It didn't. In fact, my attempts to remediate any of his academic deficits were met with combat-level resistance. In my mind, if he would only *sit down and do it* we could conquer the nightmare that was becoming school.

Nothing I did cracked the code on his learning. I decided that his deficits were either caused by emotional interference, a learning disability, poor parenting or a combination of everything.

During times of high academic stress, particularly assessments, Lee started to develop physical tics. He made sounds, involuntarily moved his lips, and made other subtle movements. We all found this curious and it heightened my awareness of the anxiety that schoolwork was creating for him.

His test scores were always below expected levels, he was often selected for interventions and extended learning programs, and he started to really hate school. Now, I didn't just have the attachment issues to work on, but the academic ones as well. Were they one and the same? I had no idea, but a family move to a new state would set the stage for an interesting experiment.

Wherever You Go, There You Are

In third grade, we moved to California, where Lee attended third through fifth grade in a small, private school. He had to pass an entrance exam, which went well. Lee's academic experience at this Carden-based school was far more suited to his strengths. He thrived in the absence of assessment-based instruction, and the small class sizes accommodated his learning style with ease. He still had to work hard, but this time he kept up on work with private teacher tutoring (all teachers offered it before and after school) and his class went on several field trips to places like the Griffith Conservatory and the California Science Center in Los Angeles. A three-day ocean excursion on a tall ship rounded out his three-year stint with his class.

This environment was so positive for Lee. We were figuring out that he was highly auditory and verbal, meaning he could learn most anything by listening and could answer questions with greater accuracy when the teacher posed them orally. Because standardized testing did not dictate his participation in a class, Lee was free and expected to learn all grade level material.

The curriculum was still rigorous and there were still times of stress (which still created tics). For example, their spelling program was based on mastering Carden Controls, which looked a little like shorthand — or dictionary pronunciation drawings. Spelling was already a challenge, so learning the words along with the controls triggered instant frustration. His aversion to reading was becoming an epic battle of wills and the piles of homework he brought home each night made me want to poke my eyes out.

It was only in third grade that Lee started to assimilate that he was different from his parents, which was both funny and startling. It was also on target with what I had learned about Korean children adopted by Caucasian parents. He started to integrate his backstory and heritage just as his academic rigor and homework increased. Third grade was the year of a fiery collision at the corner of "*I hate you!*" and "*Help me!*"

The perpetual parenting question was: *How?* How could I help?

One of the easiest and most helpful changes we made involved homework. Throughout Lee's time at Carden, the amount of homework continued to increase and escalated Lee's outbursts and behaviors. I spent hours getting him to finish assignments, and nearly died trying. What we didn't know was that homework could set up a family for misery and jeopardize already exhaustive efforts to establish and maintain a loving bond.

Homework: The Portal to Hell

When I was a special education teacher, I had the mother of a student burst through the door of my tiny resource room and demand that I talk to her. Now. She was a very tall, sturdy woman with a booming voice. She was dressed in a t-shirt and what I can only describe as plaid boxer shorts. She wore running shoes, which seemed far more sensible in that moment than my dress shoes. Running, to me, suddenly seemed like a viable and smart option.

I left the para-professional to teach the other students and calmly led the angry mom to an empty room down the hallway, passing an open-concept library where young children were perusing book shelves.

"Why does my daughter have homework? This is bullshit!" she screamed.

"I think the homework she has comes from being in the classroom. We try to work with her on homework, but she doesn't always finish it in class," I stated.

"I don't have time for this! That's why she goes to school, to do work. I don't need her doing that shit at home! She needs to do it at school! It needs to stay *here*! Don't ever send it home again!"

"Now that I know how important this is to you, I'll make sure that her work gets done here."

The actual dialogue was not that quick or efficient, although it was that heated. Many times I have thought of that mother and her daughters, who were both part of my caseload. Her youngest daughter had first arrived with long, blond hair which she used to hide her face as though behind a curtain. She wouldn't speak and refused to do anything.

With lots of hard work, the young girl eventually warmed up to us and made incredible strides before moving away two years later. When she moved, we gave her presents of Hershey nuggets (bribery was not dead and it worked in the form of Hershey nuggets) and we all cried.

I think about that mom because I believe that homework, for some of us, can be the portal to hell. If you have a child who comes home, sits down and does homework, then I want to be you in my next life.

Now that I have a far better understanding of Lee's needs, I know that homework is a hindrance to the deeper, emotional connection that my son craves (even if he doesn't think so). I didn't understand what a huge metaphor homework was for our relationship until it became the bane of my existence. When I finally heard Nancy Thomas talk about it in a conference I attended in Buffalo, Wyoming, it stuck with me for years and created an entire belief system that has alleviated so much of our suffering at home. She confirmed that schoolwork and its impact on a mother-child relationship was a recipe for failure.

She demonstrated, through her own parenting choices, that attachment issues required us to preserve the parent-child relationship at all cost. All day we are inundated with questions, arguments and other energy-draining, boundary-setting parenting tasks. Homework was an automatic trigger for Lee, due to his low tolerance for frustration, giving him the opportunity to manipulate the situation and to use learned helplessness (his feigned inability to do it himself). Sitting down to do homework prompted Lee to be clingy, whiny, demanding and manipulative. He insisted that someone sit beside him while he painstakingly did each problem. It took forever. He redirected, stalled and procrastinated like a politician on a hot-button issue. What might take other kids fifteen minutes took us *hours*. Often, violent outbursts would punctuate math and spelling assignments due the next day. I tried bribery, coaxing, cajoling, charts, reward systems and no-nonsense yelling. Nothing helped. His will was far stronger than mine. And it seemed like homework was a hill we were both willing to die on.

I started to wonder if poor parenting was really the culprit here. I knew several parents who had thrived at homeschooling. I yearned to do that for my child, to help him at home and foster his learning in a caring, non-pressured environment at his own pace, but he had no interest in learning anything from me (despite my glowing credentials and esteemed references).

In fact, the more I tried to help him with learning, the more tenuous our relationship became. My attempts to help educate him were as effective as trying to broker peace in the Middle East. It could also be that volatile. Homeschooling would have resulted in the need for an international cease fire and peace treaty — or major bodily harm to one or both of us, because I found my coping skills in those circumstances to be far less age-appropriate than my own kid's.

The worst part for me was the well-meant advice from other parents and friends. It poisoned my mind and created an extra layer of hardship in dealing with what was happening at school. At times, I was surrounded by bootstrap theorists who said they just told their kids what they wanted them to do and made them do it. Honestly, I couldn't make my child do anything. What was wrong with me? His resolve and steadfast need for control resulted in a cold war that even Ronald Reagan could not have thawed. Even so, those bootstrap theorists seemed to have good kids. I believed that I just didn't establish and hold my boundaries enough.

I watched other parents tenderly believe every word their child said and let them stay home from school when they were sick or put off their homework until morning because they were tired. Those parents seemed so loving and kind and their children were so respectful. The first time my child convinced the nurse he was sick, he skipped out of the school doors when I picked him up and asked me what we were going to do for fun. And he would have stayed home from school every single day, based on a manifested chronic illness called School Sucks-itis. But when I watched other parents being tender to their kids, I decided I wasn't loving and kind enough.

And when we went to church or visited families from our faith, I saw parents whose children spoke of God being their Heavenly Father. Those children were thoughtful, kind and well mannered. My child, from an oddly early age, told me that he didn't trust or like God because he had already made Lee have three families. I had never thought about that perspective, but it certainly made sense to me. Other children loved going to church classes and children's church, but mine rebelled and spoke ill of the Lord. I convinced myself I had not been able to teach him religion, or maybe, more accurately, I wasn't pious enough.

Basically, whatever I was doing wasn't enough.

When I fell back into my books and articles, I felt understood. It wasn't that I wasn't nice enough or pious enough. It was that my child and I were still negotiating our relationship. One that didn't start in the womb, but on the day a distressed and sad woman dropped her son off at an orphanage halfway around the world and entrusted him (eventually) to me. She had done it because she felt like there were no other options and she wanted what was best for him. What was best for him now was for me to demonstrate that I was there for him, much as an infant needs similar reassurance that someone is always there for them. Unfortunately, homework was a catalyst for discord and disrespect because he would cry *help* and I would say *try it yourself*. I was also never sure of the meaning of the teachers' exact words and instructions, which created a perfect opening for Lee to lie to and manipulate me.

We now navigate homework like the relationship invader it is. Nancy Thomas made the decision to preserve her emotional relationship with her foster children by hiring a homeschooling teacher to support them educationally. I couldn't afford to hire a homeschooling teacher, but here is what I have done instead:

- Homework is completed through after school programs, community-wide homework offerings (Boys & Girls Club) and paid tutors. I make sure very little homework comes home, because it is a guaranteed argument and will literally take *hours*. I will study with him and read with him each night, but I limit our homework when I can.

- I will type his reports and essays until he learns to type at a respectable wpm level. Until then, my typing for him made my involvement about the method and not the writing content.

- If a homework task seems redundant (like doing a study sheet and writing notecards with the same information), I will ask the teacher if we can skip one or the other so we can spend more time studying orally and less time reinforcing his poor and inaccurate handwriting skills. Now that Lee has been diagnosed with unique vision issues, we know for sure that writing is an ineffective way for him to learn and retain material.

- I let it go. There are times when homework comes home to be finished. If he forgets, I let him forget.

- I make sure to be in contact with all of his teachers so that if homework is missing, I am made aware of it and can arrange for him to catch up with the help of a tutor or at the next extended learning opportunity.

Slowly, I incorporated what I was learning through various resources and was starting to get a better picture of what parenting a child with adverse childhood experiences was like and what it took support that kind of kid.

The dichotomy of home and school blended to create unique and enduring behaviors that were becoming more volatile as he got older, but we were making progress. Mitigating homework created a deep relief for me and was one of many interventions we were using to help us manage deep feelings. Since working with the school on the issue of homework had made such an impact, I was more motivated than ever to make sure they understood our plight and continued to act as an ally in supporting Lee.

SECTION TWO

LESSONS ON FINDING HELP

"That we accept the world as it is does not in any sense weaken our desire to change it into what we believe it should be — it is necessary to begin where the world is if we are going to change it to what we think it should be. That means working in the system."

Saul D. Alinsky

RULES FOR RADICALS

CHAPTER THREE

Working with the School

Every fall at our house, the resistance begins. Lee denounces school and is completely uninterested in shopping for supplies. While most parents and children seem to bond over the build-up to the first day of school, my child bans the word "school" from being uttered. I drag him to the store and ogle over new mechanical pencils and cool math gear. He thinks I am insane and looks as interested as I would be at a craft convention. Last year, we shopped directly from the school supply list in less than 45 minutes (this year, it was a whopping 20 minutes!). I helped him set up a few binders and made sure he had the basics. It was anticlimactic for a girl like me, who is addicted to office supplies and the belief that a new fall wardrobe is imperative for survival.

I knew the educational landscape had changed radically since I had traded teaching for homemaking over a decade ago. When I first started teaching, the classroom curriculum was far more student-centered. Student inquiry was part of the lessons and students were evaluated in a variety of ways including essays, teacher-made tests, presentations and hands-on projects. The lessons and outcomes lent themselves to all learning styles, without the worry of standardized guidelines and test rankings. But the educational landscape is constantly changing.

Lee, who had thrived in a private educational environment where his auditory and verbal learning preferences could be effortlessly accommodated, found himself straightjacketed by the expectations and rankings of regularly administered assessments once he returned to Wyoming public education in sixth grade.

In some districts, frustration comes from a lack of resources. In our case, there was a crisis of abundance. I know: abundance of resources doesn't seem like it would be a problem. But it was for us.

Our school district, rife with resources, offered instructional interventions, differentiated learning, extended school learning opportunities and leveled tiers of restricted learning environments in order to ensure student success. I agree that educational assistance is effective and useful, but there comes a point at which this concept is a reinforcement of a student's limitations and perpetuates the ever-present core belief of failure.

Junior high is always a bit of a question mark. I think the parents are more nervous than the kids. There is a lot to consider, the schedule is harder to navigate and, well, it's junior high. Just dealing with my own remembered teenage angst was enough to make me cringe. Moving from the cocoon of elementary to unbridled chaos with a myriad of other students would be daunting to anyone. The fun part was picking a locker-mate and electives. But, for Lee, the fun part was curtailed by his sixth-grade standardized test scores.

Based solely on his score for the Measures of Academic Progress (MAP) test, our son was invited to a research-based supplemental reading class. The formal invitation that arrived at our residence made this class sound like the cure to all of Lee's reading problems. My husband was all in.

I eyed the letter cautiously and considered rejecting the invitation. That's the peril of having a special education background and having worked in the school district; I had extensive background knowledge on various programs. Here's what I knew: This was a computer-based reading intervention similar to one our district used at the early elementary level. Lee had already been exposed to that program (amongst several others) throughout his school career. None of the interventions implemented to date had miraculously cured our son of low reading scores.

My inner special educator wondered how this method would be different. If we were talking about dealing with a true learning disability, like dyslexia, which was becoming more and more evident to me as a possibility, I was aware that typical intervention strategies would not fix the problem. Furthermore, I wondered about the emotional impact of yet another intervention, Lee being separated from his peers and then giving up an elective. Our lifelong theme of finding balance between helping and defeating is a very delicate one.

Since my husband was still on board the miracle reading train, I agreed to set up a meeting with the reading coordinator at the school. She touted the benefits of the program and showed us proof of dramatic student progress. Some students were even dismissed from this program because their reading scores shot up to grade level. It was hard to argue with her enthusiasm and data. We enrolled Lee in the class on the slight chance that this was it, the miracle that would finally crack the code on his reading and make his life grand. I also agreed because I didn't want to be wrong if he did, in fact, see benefits from this class.

One elective was gone. He would now have to keep up in a regular English class and attend the intervention reading class. To his credit, like the rest of us, he resigned himself to yet another offering that he hoped would work. Maybe this would make him a better student so that he wouldn't have to keep trying so hard to be a typical kid without struggles.

What I had really wanted was a study hall for Lee. I wanted an elective where he could keep up on homework with a live person who could monitor and help him as needed. From my previous work with the district, I knew this existed in some form at his school, so I asked for it preemptively during the reading meeting. School personnel insisted it did not exist. I dropped it. Obviously, it was not available upon request.

What was available was a before- and after-school "extended learning opportunity." A few weeks into his junior high career, Lee was invited to attend as a result of unfinished classwork and several forgotten homework assignments. If there is one thing he is good at, it's securing invitations to supportive educational opportunities.

The woman running the program was mean (according to Lee). I happened to love her. She knew every assignment he had due, made sure he finished them before coming home, and when he forgot to bring his half-finished worksheets, she conveniently had him start anew from the stash in her desk. She was the kind of woman who made life at home easier. She also knew to follow up with me when Lee had not quite finished a task, because homework and study materials mysteriously vanished between the final bell and home. His backpack must have been a portable Bermuda Triangle.

By November, the school team had met about Lee. I have no proof that is what happened, but I've been a teacher and know that there are many meetings and an abundance of strategy sessions all done in the name of our children. Regardless of how it happened, Lee was invited to the secret study hall! The only drawback to joining secret study hall was that he would have to leave a health class in which they discussed diet, exercise and healthy choices. It was not part of the core curriculum, but given the way that kid craves fast food, I felt he needed to hear about the negative effects of eating chicken nuggets and French fries with wild adolescent abandon, as he did far too often.

Desperate for the study hall, I threw nuggets to the wind and signed him up. He was now the proud invitee to a special reading class, extended school hours, and a secret study hall. He had an abundance of assistance and I was so grateful. But for all the gratitude, there was the slightest bit of resentment and sadness. He was also a kid with a fierce need to fit in, and the interventions countered his deep need to appear typical.

A few short weeks later, the school called again. Lee was invited to a supplemental math class along with his core math class. I revealed that we had hired a private tutor (a friend and former teacher) and declined the invitation. I could not subject him to one more intervention or take away another elective.

A little of my soul left my body. The invitations for help were becoming overkill. Each day, Lee crashed through the door like a pirate on peyote: bloodshot eyes, a wobbly gait, his body slumped in fatigue. Every day he looked like he had been through a war. Every. Single. Day. In fact, he would often fall asleep on the couch once he had satisfied his bottomless adolescent belly.

And it wasn't because he was tired. Lee retired every night by 9 pm. Sometimes he fell asleep at 7 pm. Most nights by 8 pm he was on autopilot, capable of no work and no rational thought. It made for impossible late-night homework stints and battles to brush his teeth.

I was convinced that the amount of effort it took for Lee to get through his day at school was proportional to someone climbing to the top of Mount Everest. Following along, listening intently, writing things down and figuring out social cues absolutely drained him. It was hard for me not to feel sorry for him every night. With core academic and additional supplemental classes all day long, it's no wonder he referred to school as Alcatraz. We had visited Alcatraz when we lived in California and it paints a very bleak picture. He was fully aware of the comparison.

It's not a good feeling to send your child to a place you know highlights his weaknesses day after day. It's not intentional, but every test score that falls short and every supplemental class he attends sends a message. He knows his test scores are always low. He knows he is singled out to work more on the very tasks he hates, but he is persistent and reliable. I worry, though. I wonder how much he resigns himself to never being enough. I wonder how much school confirms the worthlessness he feels. I wonder how much he will endure before he gives up and doesn't want to do it anymore. I wonder how to equal out the torment of this academic and emotional strife.

At the end of his first year in junior high I took stock of what we had learned. In the end, the abundance of interventions and support were almost a burden. It resulted in something akin to oppression from learning the general curriculum (which he had managed well in a private school setting) and segregation from his typical peers while attending supplemental and support classes. It seemed like his differences were emphasized at every turn, which is doubly difficult for an insecure, attachment-affected kid just trying to fit in and be liked by others. But it became clear that while there were imperfections and tough decisions to be made, follow through was just a result of working within a system.

More importantly, when it came to Lee's education, there had been goodness. When I looked back, I realized that every single year since he had started school, he had a teacher encourage him and cheer him on. His teachers have accommodated, listened to and communicated with me beyond the scope of what is required. Principals and administrators have made time to hear me out (even though they have plenty to do and I'm talking to them about theories and policies they can't change).

I finally grasped what the school system was to us. It was a place that provided opportunities and choices, and had many working parts. Driving home one day, I understood that with a little persistence and a willingness to collaborate, I had created a network of caring individuals who were willing to help us wade through yet another year. It turned out that school, to some extent, was a result of what I was willing to create.

School as a System

The basic definition of a system is a set of connected things or parts forming a complex whole. It became helpful for me to remember that our school districts, like our health and legal systems, are systems, too. Systems can seem impersonal, inefficient, frustrating at times and highly regulated. The good news is that school systems consist of many individuals who care about children. There are always exceptions, but the quality of the school personnel I have met and worked with as a parent and over my career as a teacher indicates that not many people get up and report to work with the intent to do harm.

Think about a system you already know and can navigate with ease. For example, you may be an accountant who can guide anyone through a complicated tax return with your eyes closed. Or you may file insurance for a local physician or dentist, meaning you understand the processes and codes associated with our increasingly complex health care system. Just knowing about a system puts you at an advantage because you understand which rules are fixed and where exceptions can be made. Our knowledge of and experience with a certain system is the foundation for how we begin to interact with that particular system.

Think back to your earliest experiences with school. What sensations and thoughts come up for you? Was it challenging? Easy? What were your teachers like? Did you like your teachers? Your principal? Did you have lots of friends? Did you get good grades?

The reason it's important to honestly acknowledge what school was like for you is because it informs the way you will approach the system and the people in it now. Consider my early experiences with dentists. When I was very young, my mother would drive us 45 miles to the nearest dentist. Inevitably, thanks to my weak teeth, I would have cavities. Rather than return to the dentist another day, my mother agreed that he could fill those cavities immediately, all at once. It was probably very convenient for my mother, but was awfully painful and distressing for me. The dread was palpable every time we saddled up for a trip to the dentist. My siblings never had cavities!

My mother, in an attempt to ease my suffering, would offer to take me to the local department store where I could buy a velour contoured coloring poster as a peace offering. It didn't make it better. When I had to have cavities filled as an adult, I would take the entire afternoon off of work to snuggle on the couch, watch daytime television and recover. My youthful dentistry experience has consistently shaped my adult dental experiences. I am not a good patient and am often skeptical and condescending when I speak to dental professionals. I'm not proud of that.

Years after my early dentist trauma, Lee arrived from Korea in need of much dental work. Finding a pediatric dentist and watching Lee go through so many procedures has triggered some kind of post-traumatic dental syndrome for me. Lee is far braver than I am. In fact, when his four front baby teeth had to be extracted, I was nearly apoplectic. I felt it was a reflection on me and insisted that he fill the empty space with a bridge — fake baby teeth that made him look like other kids his age. He was still two to three years out from losing his baby teeth. Lee hated that thing. He constantly wiggled it out and I finally gave up on keeping it in. He was fine without it.

Over the years, Lee and I have been to the dentist and orthodontist many times. He has had teeth extracted, root canals done, cavities filled, and braces put on and adjusted. Just as I did when I was a child, I still get anxious when I walk into the waiting room. And just as my childhood experiences continue to affect our current dental visits (we are now extracting wisdom teeth!), so will your previous school experiences affect the way you approach the school when partnering in your child's education. Without noticing the baggage we carry from our early years, we unconsciously risk foisting that negative perception onto whatever is happening, which can jeopardize our ability to work within the school.

One realization that has helped me is acknowledging that the educational delivery system is formed by layers of federal, state and local systems. Having worked with students with disabilities, I know my staff came to school every day with the intention of making a difference and doing the best they could to teach every student. They often worked extra hours, spent their own money on classroom supplies, and attended all required professional development and staff meetings. As regimented as I was about implementing every aspect of every individualized education plan (IEP) under my supervision, there were inevitable gaps and circumstances beyond my control. Even the most conscientious well-intentioned teacher or administrator can occasionally fail.

What I have learned over and over is that I create more suffering for myself (and, by extension, for my child) when I thrust all of my expectations unilaterally on the school and its professionals to fulfill. The more responsibility I take for what happens at school, the more involved and empowered I feel.

I have gained so much parental empowerment from assuming an active role as my child's advocate. I am no longer frustrated when plans go awry or I find out my child is missing five assignments. In becoming a partner, I take full responsibility for the choices I make on behalf of Lee. I can accept that even the best-laid plans don't always work out and that Lee bears accountability as well. I now anticipate that advocating for Lee is not a passive endeavor with sporadic calls to action through loud protests wielding a pitchfork, but a constant assessment of what is happening now and what needs to change in the immediate future to be helpful. With a child in need of academic and emotional support, like Lee, I've learned that working with the school becomes a masterful balance between advocating, guiding and letting go.

Considerations for Working With the School

Research the Best Fit for You and Your Child

As I mentioned before, I would have liked to homeschool Lee. I think it would have protected his ego from the constant barrage of subliminal negative messages he receives at school through test scores, grades and comments about lack of organization (which is admittedly disconcerting). I have also considered enrolling him in a virtual school, although most of them are structured much like homeschool and have the added "bonus" of requiring computer skills. Again, Lee has not been on the forefront of computer engineering — or even using a keyboard.

My other option was to consider a private school in our area, but the class size was too small. I know that may sound counterintuitive, but if a class of ten children is academically above average, then his deficits are even more prominent in comparison. At least in public school, the range of abilities is far more forgiving.

Therefore, our family's choice was public school, given our situation and geographic location. In your case, a private or specialized school may fit the bill. Don't be afraid to explore. There are also several online options that may be appealing to your family, too. I know children who happily combine virtual and public schools.

In this day and age, the options are endless. Make the choice based on where you live, what options are available and what is best for your family. Once you've made the decision, commit to it. The unknown can be frightening, but often a commitment to your values and decisions can prove rewarding in the end.

Be an Active Part of the Team

Whether your child is struggling academically, behaviorally or both, consider yourself an integral part of the school team. Parents have been known to view school personnel as adversaries, but I have discovered that a little effort can go a long way. Remember when I said that the whole team had a meeting about Lee before offering him the secret study hall? In some cases, it happens that teachers talk. That can feel confusing for parents and set up an "us" versus "them" mentality. If you can, consider it from an angle of compassion. Staff personnel do engage in casual conversations, and sometimes more formal discussions, about students. Typically, these conversations are to consider thoughtful and helpful interventions for your child. Even though I know the discussions are useful and necessary, as a parent I catch myself feeling left out and sometimes angry that people talk about my kid behind my back. I already feel a need to protect my child from so much. And I know so much more about my child; why don't they just ask me?

Teachers do want our input. When they engage in banter about our kids they are trying to come up with solutions or new ideas. Much like you bounce ideas about finances, parenting or vacation plans off of your spouse, so do teachers seek advice and ideas on students they see struggling. It is not a vindictive form of slander or mean-spirited cackling, but rather a genuine inquiry as to how to increase a child's educational experience. They want our children to succeed, and most are willing to do anything to help.

As part of the team, know that you may ask to meet with any teachers, administrators, counselors or specialists at any time. I have never been refused a request to meet with a teacher. In most cases, they are eternally grateful for my ideas and are happy to know they can call me anytime. When you show an interest in working with the team or a teacher and believe that they are there to do likewise, the experience can open doors of communication and cooperation that will last as long as your child resides in that school. It also helps to let them know you are open to hearing from them, too!

Set Yourself Up for Success

Each year, our children typically move on to new teachers. And each year, I prepare and update a Parent Information Sheet for my child's teacher. I will usually set up a one-on-one meeting time the second or third week of school, after the excitement wanes and a regular routine emerges. I will either email an advance copy or bring my information sheet to leave with Lee's new teacher. This small gesture has never failed me, especially when Lee was in elementary school. Consider the meeting a preemptive strike or a first date.

The point of my meeting is not only to share my son's strengths, weaknesses and background, but to visit candidly and casually with the teacher. While she likely won't remember everything I have said to her or digest all of my information, she will appreciate the time I spend with her and we will have had a nice visit. Informal meetings often give me a sense of how the teacher likes to communicate and the tone with which she does it (some are more formal and others appreciate my sense of humor). From that point on, I keep in touch through regular emails and phone calls so that if anything should come up during the year I am not a stranger and they will not hesitate to call.

Remember in first grade when Lee was caught cheating on a spelling test? His teacher was a new recruit in our district and my first communication from her was that Lee had to stay after school for detention. I was mortified and a little upset that this poor kid was being punished for reacting to an unprecedented situation that had created high anxiety. I also surmised through our conversation that she had made an example of him in front of the class. I had two choices: I could eat her for lunch like a momma bear protecting her young or I could try to work with it. I chose to work with it.

I let her take care of the situation in the manner she saw fit. I also prepared my first information sheet and set up a meeting with her. I shared pertinent background information, talked about why Lee may have reacted the way he did during the spelling pretest, and gently suggested ideas for helping him in class. She was highly receptive to my efforts.

You'll recall that first grade had some rough patches. Each time I started to have anxiety about Lee's school career, I would call his teacher and we would work through it together. She became my biggest ally and one of his favorite teachers. We even went to her wedding that summer. I think back to that first week and wonder what might have been, had I chosen an alternate path. I am so glad we gave each other the benefit of the doubt and worked to create a collaborative relationship.

Conversely, in sixth grade, I perceived Lee's teacher to be inexplicably cool and aloof. As always, I met with her and presented my information. She was receptive, but I could tell there wasn't a personal connection. I continued with intermittent phone calls and emails throughout the year. She told me she would write in his planner each night and make sure Lee put the planner in his backpack at the end of the day and got it out each morning. By November he had lost the planner for good. Despite my requests, it was never replaced and communication stopped. However, the teacher did make accommodations for him and I suspect she worked harder in class with him than I gave her credit for, because she was always respectful of my input. Educationally, that was not his best year, but I did learn some valuable lessons, despite my frustration. It stretched me to consider life beyond the classroom. I had to surrender daily control of Lee's education and decide when it was important to speak up. I also reminded myself that our children grow and become stronger through adversity. And, frankly, I'm not even sure that Lee felt things were adverse. That may have just been me.

Setting myself up for success by visiting candidly and purposefully with teachers has afforded me so much support over the years. Not every teacher has become a lifelong friend, but many have.

Find Your People

As you may have deducted from what I said about the sixth grade teacher, not everyone on your child's team is going to be your cup of tea. You may have to discern allies from acquaintances.

One time, excited about what I had learned from Nancy Thomas about attachment and post-traumatic stress, I scheduled a session with the school counselor. To me, the information was fascinating and every counselor should know about it. My secret hope was that she would be enraptured by this revolutionary research and meet with my child to help him overcome anxiety, gain independence and better his social skills. None of that happened.

The school counselor politely let me speak for many uninterrupted minutes. When I was finished with my mini-lesson, she reached into her desk and handed me some forms to fill out. She suggested I take them home and collaborate with my husband and return them. I was agog. She had given me attention deficit hyperactivity disorder (ADHD) and attention deficit disorder (ADD) rating scales! These rating scales are often used as part of an elaborate protocol to determine if a child has ADHD or ADD. These diagnoses are very appropriate in some circumstances, but I had just spent the last fifteen minutes telling her that symptoms of attachment and post-traumatic stress often mirror ADHD/ADD and that I wanted her to work with my child to mitigate some of the mild behaviors that were emerging, like stealing compact paint palettes from the art room or broken pieces of pen from classroom floors. It was clear she was not buying what I was selling that day.

Deflated, I accepted the questionnaires and thanked her for her time. She had taught me who she was in that moment and I had to believe her. She was a counselor who knew a lot about ADHD and ADD, mostly because of the swell of students diagnosed over the past few years. I knew the statistics and the protocols from having been a case manager and facilitating these evaluations in the past. She had her beliefs and I had mine. She just wasn't my people.

Finding your people requires being open to a larger sphere of helpers. Think creatively and actively seek the support of personnel who believe in your child and with whom you are comfortable talking and problem-solving. Whether it's a counselor, teacher or specialist (music teacher, occupational therapist, principal), seek advice and assistance from them as needed. A supportive and understanding school staff member can help you more comfortably navigate the system and help you feel less isolated.

Enlist an Advocate

Being an advocate for your child can be exhausting, especially if you are dealing with a situation like mine at home. Not many people know how tumultuous and draining family life can be with a child who has had adverse early experiences.

No matter how compassionate people are or how much they may say they understand our predicaments, no one can embrace the essence of what home is like for parents raising children with attachment issues. Even more to the point, no one can truly appreciate the fortitude, energy and demands placed on the mother of such a family.

That is why I strongly suggest that parents bring their own advocate or friend to any meeting involving their child. When a devastating medical diagnosis befalls a loved one, the medical community encourages bringing an extra set of ears to help listen, remember and record what is discussed. Highly charged meetings can have a similarly disorienting effect on a parent who's feeling the everyday fatigue and overwhelm of parenting and life. Enlisting an extra set of ears and a calming presence can be highly effective in getting what you need while remaining an integral part of the school system's team.

Bringing such people to a meeting is a great idea, but intention makes a huge difference. If we bring along someone to be a comrade-in-arms for an adversarial position, the atmosphere will most certainly be adversarial.

But what if you see yourself as part of the team and no one has to win or lose?

When I was a teacher and case manager, I conducted my share of meetings. I still look back fondly on meetings in which families brought an advocate, or when state lawyers were involved. When an impartial attendee sits in on a meeting, everyone makes an extra effort to keep their emotions in check. It's not unlike coming to Thanksgiving Dinner and having the local parish priest in attendance. No one wants to air their family's dirty laundry while the priest is there eating Mom's green bean casserole!

No one loves you like your mom. And no one feels the heartache of having a child who struggles more than a mom. In the name of all things holy, we just want our kids to be okay, accepted and happy.

Sadly, navigating the world of education can feel like a huge kick in the stomach. Ultimately, we are asking a child to fit into a rigid system that amplifies all the ways in which he may not fit. And then we are reminded of all the ways we wish things were different for our struggling children. And by wishing things were different or working tirelessly to make them different, we experience deep suffering. No system can assuage that kind of abiding love and sorrow. Grief and heartache are inherently part of the package. And they are triggers for me in any meeting or whenever I deal with school personnel.

What has made it a little easier for me to accept is that not every school day will be perfect and there is likely no school panacea that will cure Lee of his learning deficits. Instead, I remind myself that our journeys are meant for us and we will prevail, despite any challenges we face together. My painful future projections hijack my appreciation of what is happening now.

So, if you find yourself crying in your car before a school meeting because it's been a rough week and you can't bear to hear one more negative thing about your child, take heart. I have been there more than once. It's rather cathartic, and I keep a stash of gummy bears in my glove compartment for added support.

Three Ultimate Questions

When I first read *How to Read a Book: The Classic Guide to Intelligent Reading* by Mortimer J. Adler and Charles Van Doren, I was struck by the obvious concept that every book is best read in context. Their methods for reading a book reminded me not just to consider the context of the story, but the era in which it was written and any pertinent information about the author. There are so many filters and lenses that create a story. It's not unlike this story I am telling now, through the lens of an adoptive mother in midlife reflecting on a particularly impressionable parenting journey. There are so many ingredients that go into my parenting story.

The same thing is true for anything that happens in school. The lenses through which we view a perceived or actual problem are many. Most often, I choose to panic first. I usually jump to the worst-case scenario and have a little meltdown before getting hold of my good sense. With time (and lots of deep breathing), I can slowly see the situation for the opportunity it is to create a better version of what I need. I have devised an entire process out of the following three questions. This process helps me to consider what I want versus what I need, and what my real purpose is in this odyssey we call education.

I first heard the three questions in a crackling staccato by a lanky junior high student with dark hair, a sharp wit and a mischievous glint in his eye. He came to my classroom daily for homework help and was never particularly thrilled to be there. I'm pretty sure school was not his jam, but we made the best of it.

The thing that impressed me most about this young man was his natural way of being. His essence was clear. He was an outdoorsman, didn't mince words and knew what he liked — and what he didn't. He was also very kind and genuine. At least, that's what I remember from all those years ago.

The deadpan delivery of his questioning started out of the blue one day and continued for as long as I can remember. Each time a student would wander into my resource room, we all heard his famous tag line: *Whaddya want? Whaddya need? Whaddya here for?* The questions were meant literally and prompted every newcomer to state their intention as soon as they entered my classroom. He reminded me of a mythical sphinx — a waiting predator posing an unanswerable riddle to every passerby. He never really cared about your answer though; he just liked to pose the questions.

From what I hear, he grew into quite a young man, with the same passion for nature and doing the things he loved. Sadly, he died in a skydiving accident just a few years ago. I don't know this for sure, but I like to think he probably knew all along what he wanted, what he needed and what he was here for. Now, when I encounter a situation with my son I allow myself space to react and then I settle into my process by asking myself three questions that have left an indelible mark on my soul.

What do I want?

Usually I will pull out my journal and draft a letter about the offending party or situation. An uncensored written rant usually reveals what I inherently want. What I typically want is: not to deal with a hard situation and for my child (or me) to be perfect and without hardship. The list can go on.

Journaling about what is bothering me and what I want allows a release of emotion. For example, when the study hall class was not as productive as I had hoped, I was exasperated. Lee was already involved in a myriad of interventions and he was missing a curriculum class for the promise of a stellar study hall. I was bothered that this was touted as a level 2 intervention, even though it was not as effective as other programming options, in my opinion. The more I learned and thought about it, the more upset I became. I was inherently mad because I just wanted Lee to have a smooth schedule, one that didn't involve special classes and a heap of collaboration with different teachers. I wanted our school experience to be easy and normal. I wanted the teacher to be compassionate towards my plight.

What do I need?

If what I want is steeped in perfection and expectation, then what I need is a reasonable outcome for optimizing the current situation for all of us. I have to acknowledge my limited sphere of control and work within the system. In my study hall example, I needed it to be a place where work was completed despite Lee's lack of organization and independent work ethic. I knew I had several choices, but the end result needed to be minimal work sent home.

My first idea was to reach out to the study hall teacher. She explained her situation. She had double duty during Lee's study hall time, did not have access to classroom materials (which was a perfect opportunity for Lee to be "forgetful" and so have to do less homework), and her philosophy was that the kids needed to bring all of their materials with them and complete their work independently. If work wasn't done in study hall, it was sent home to be done. In some ways, her philosophy felt counterintuitive to Lee's needs. If he failed to arrive prepared or to work independently, his time was wasted and he brought the work home (most of which sat crumpled in the bottom of his backpack because I didn't know it was there).

I first had to accept that this study hall system had been in place for decades. As a study hall teacher, Ms. Xavier knew what worked for her. And just because it didn't fit my needs and expectations did not mean it was wrong or egregiously harmful to my child. She likely had no background information about Lee, nor did she understand my needs. After we talked and I gently filled her in on my concerns and Lee's background, there was mutual understanding. Within months, we were emailing daily, she was monitoring his work and would let me know if work had to come home. When work started coming home regularly, we sent Lee back to the extended learning lab to complete his homework there. Were those long days? Yes, but the integrity of our evening relationship and his deep need to unwind at home were honored through effortful communication with the teacher and the knowledge that I always had options.

I have also had conversations with several moms about receiving regular phone calls from school. Most of the time, their child is on the line confessing a transgression. Moms have often lamented to me about these frequent call situations. On the one hand, a partnership with the school is a huge advantage in addressing behaviors. Conversely, it seems like a barrage of bad news can create a stress response every time the phone rings, like a twisted Pavlovian experiment.

Usually what moms want is for the child to behave, follow rules and for the school to stop phoning the overwhelmed parent so frequently. The need is to address the communication style and set parameters that are effective. If you are feeling overwhelmed with phone calls that don't seem to be working, ask for notes to be sent home or for your child to write a confession instead. Emails may even reduce the sting of phone calls. The options are limitless if we focus on solutions, which is more about what we need than what we ultimately want.

What am I here for?

I am here to advocate for my child, which means I have the delicate job of simultaneously building and preserving a relationship while fostering my son's independence. This is no easy task when your child struggles to fit in. My instinct is to protect him rather than allow lessons and opportunities for growth.

In considering my role as parent and advocate, I have learned to separate two very different intentions when I interact with the school system or any system. I consider carefully what I am able to change now versus what theoretical injustice I want to fix (like too much standardized testing). This distinction allows me to spare busy administrators my lengthy diatribes and esoteric rants so that we can focus on what is happening in the classroom rather than on a separate, more philosophical picture.

I stop myself immediately when I think, "Well, they should...."

Because the school system is just that: a system with a specific purpose, which is to educate a great number of children in the most effective way. It is not responsible for fixing or curing my child. When I set the expectation that the school is responsible for all aspects of teaching and improving my child, disappointment is inevitable.

Once I figured out how to balance my own needs and wants in dealing with the school, I then had to get clear on how to best help Lee handle the big feelings that were coming home as the result of messages he was receiving in school and from the world at large. How could I empower myself as a mom to help guide Lee through the grueling days spent academically toiling and navigating complex social strata?

Therapeutic parenting helped us understand a new way of parenting that didn't necessarily cure every ill, but did give us the impetus to parent more compassionately, which slowly started to release the power struggles and tensions that had plagued us in the early years.

CHAPTER FOUR

Home Is Where the Hardship Is

One of my favorite quotes of all time is this: *I walk around like everything is fine, but deep down, inside my shoe, my sock is falling off.* I don't know its author, but it sums up my parenting experience nicely. I have spent a lot of energy keeping it together and appearing as put-together as my mom friends, but there have been days, between the hardships of school and home, when, deep inside, I have questioned if I could hang on.

No one knows what happens behind closed doors. Behind those doors, everyone is living their own story. In the case of a child with early adverse experiences, home can be one of the most difficult places for every single family member.

Inside the safety of our home is where Lee lets down his guard. Inside our home's walls, his threshold for tolerance and frustration was very low, triggering major blow-ups at the mention of school, a common household chore or a change in plans. These outbursts, worthy of a Richter scale rating, were usually delayed reactions to what he perceived as daily injustices, such as kids calling him names (sometimes racial), or a teacher making him do something he thought was impossible, or someone simply cutting in front of him in the lunch line. Every injustice, no matter how slight, confirmed Lee's view that nothing ever worked out for him. I have observed this pervasive belief ever since he was young enough to interact with the world. I find it odd and interesting that a child so young could be so certain of life's repeated negative outcomes. He had had so little life experience before taking on that belief. However, he had lived a lot of life in his short years and those experiences had undoubtedly contributed to his defeatist attitude.

As a mom, his negativity and my need for him to be different was a tough dichotomy to navigate. My hope was that he would ultimately understand that his view of the world perpetuated his experiences, but it was hard to argue that, for him, his conclusion was reasonable to have come to, given his experiences thus far. The tricky part was balancing his right to experience his feelings against the knowledge that his past didn't have to define his life forevermore. I was hoping my education, experience and intuition would help him channel his inner Rumi.

I buoyed my spirits by reminding myself I was the oldest of five kids, had been babysitting since junior high, held a degree in education and taught special education students in the public school system. I had a vast array of tools in my parenting toolbox. Ladies and gentlemen, I had mad street cred when it came to parenting and child development.

Furthermore, as part of my undergraduate degree, I had taken an entire semester on behavior modification, during which I had designed elaborate charts and systems aimed at extinguishing undesirable behaviors. I had implemented the improvement plans while managing the inevitable uptick in those undesirable behaviors until they slowly waned over time. Through charting and perseverance, it was proven that even the most intense behaviors could be taught or eradicated.

As a teacher, I had attended several conferences and seminars addressing behavior management in the classroom. I knew the finer points of positive, negative and intermittent reinforcement. I completed a three-day intensive training on functional behavior assessments designed to observe, record and analyze behaviors, with the sole purpose of finding out why a behavior existed and what to do about it. I also taught positive parenting classes in our community.

I felt highly qualified to parent a child. But even with the tools I had, I felt lost at times. How could I feel so defeated every single day? Why did I feel so helpless?

While I considered Lee's toddler experiences important and impactful, I had not considered how these early experiences informed his beliefs and behaviors. The answer was in our *relationship*.

When Past Becomes Present

When I tell people that Lee is adopted, they often ask how old he was when he came home. I typically respond with the truth, that he was almost two years old. Many people replied, "Oh, so he wasn't old enough to remember," as though convincing themselves that a child so young would have no memory of his past and thus early experiences could not leave lingering emotional effects.

I love the metaphor evoked by a recent study conducted by Martha Weiss of Georgetown University, in which she demonstrated that moths remember information and make connections from when they were caterpillars. Weiss and her colleagues exposed tobacco hornworm caterpillars to a pungent odor (like my preteen's socks, perhaps?). After the caterpillar metamorphosed into a moth, over 75% of the time the airborne insect indicated an aversion to the same pungent chemical they had been exposed to as caterpillars, leading scientists to conclude that the moths remembered their early experiences as caterpillars.

The most intriguing part of this experiment is that, while in its metamorphic stage, every part of a caterpillar, including its brain, literally dissolves into a gooey substance that is completely restructured into a moth or butterfly. What a powerful way to suggest that what happens to us as children is imprinted into our brains and carried forward! Many people assume that if you can't articulate a memory, then it won't have any residual effects. Science now shows that we are highly impressionable, especially as developing infants learning about the world.

Emerging brain research and this metamorphic phenomenon convinced me of the need for a different parenting approach. Most mainstream parenting paradigms assume that there is a secure and enduring bond between parent and child. Most typical children would have to work very hard to jeopardize that bond. But when we parent or step-parent a child who has experienced adverse childhood circumstances, that secure attachment and enduring bond may not yet be established or secure.

Therefore, it made sense to me that my parenting responses had to simultaneously teach life lessons and offer correction while continuing to establish and protect a bond that was not yet internalized. Because Lee had experienced multiple primary caregiver disruptions at a critical stage of development, I believed it was imperative to parent him through that unique lens, providing typical parental expectations while still taking care to guard the emerging relationship. For other kids with secure, more typically formed attachments, behaviors did not necessarily carry the same messages and meaning as they did for Lee and other kids like him.

This was the main insight I gained from the local conference with Nancy Thomas. She illustrated perfectly that in order to establish a secure bond, the question my son needed answered with unmistakable regularity was: *Can you keep me safe?* This question is thought to be at the core of every behavior for a child who has had a difficult beginning. The theory is that a child's behavior is meant to determine if and when their world would be completely upended again. It would have been handy if Lee could have just asked me if I could keep him safe. Instead, he was repeatedly asking me in more subtle ways. He inquired (through his behavior) and then determined the answer by how I responded (through my behavior). Finally, perceived parental ineffectiveness made sense. I had been failing Lee's tests.

One of the most basic examples I can think of to illustrate this point is hugging. We all hug our children. It is intuitive. According to research, hugging releases feel-good hormones. Who knew it was also used to establish personal power and respect? For healing souls like Lee, hugging correctly is therapeutic. It involves flat hands on the back, a heart to heart stance and a gentle squeeze with the leader's (or parent's) arms on top.

I tried hugging Lee therapeutically shortly after I returned from the conference. To my surprise, when I placed my arms on top of his in the leadership position, he instinctively jockeyed for his to be on top. I was fascinated by his reflex to unconsciously take charge, and even more convinced that specialized parenting techniques for children with adverse experiences might be more effective and create a more peaceful home environment. When I discovered new ways of observing my child's needs, by identifying the driving reasons behind his behaviors, the nuances helped me parent with greater compassion.

For example, consider how much children interrupt. Every child interrupts, and eventually learns that interrupting is not acceptable. As they grow, they may learn to engage in self-play when redirected, or simply learn to wait patiently. Children with attachment issues consider it their mission in life to see how often they can successfully interrupt you. It can be an impressive assault and should be deemed inhumane by the Geneva Convention. However, this kind of persistence is necessary when you consider its underlying cause. Simply stated, if a child with an insecure attachment can succeed in drawing you away from whatever you are doing to engage with them for even a second, they are calculating how strong you would be if someone walked in and attempted to take them away. To typical parents, this may sound like a ridiculous over-analysis of a simple typical behavior. Granted, there are many reasons why children interrupt. But for those of us with children who are insecure in their attachment, our parenting behaviors need to show that we are the leaders who will keep them safe now and forever. The stakes feel huge, which is why it can feel so daunting when things are falling apart.

When I read *Building the Bonds of Attachment* by attachment specialist Daniel Hughes, I was riveted. This book chronicles an indefatigable foster parent and her attempts to therapeutically parent a child with severe attachment deficits. While the book's extreme circumstances did not reflect our personal, milder experiences, they did convey the emotional toll of parenting a child with consistently challenging behaviors. During one scene in the book, the foster mother and her entire family decided to attend Thanksgiving dinner at her parents' house. The subtle and subversive ways the foster child manipulated the situation led to harsh judgment of the foster mother and a breakdown of family support and empathy for this mom who was giving everything. I wept when I read this passage, not because I was living it, but because the mother's subsequent exasperation and defeat in the aftermath was palpable. I had honestly felt that defeated and alone at times. I felt like that when Ellen blandly accepted my apology for her perception of my poor parenting. I felt that way when Lee was stealing repeatedly in the first grade and I didn't know what to do about it. Those were moments in which I could not adequately convey my hopelessness in words.

Finding Hope

As we continued our quest for more peaceful parenting, my husband and I learned more and more about therapeutic parenting. I had learned a lot from reading the likes of Daniel Hughes, Nancy Thomas and Denise Best, Licensed Professional Counselor (LPC) specializing in attachment, trauma and therapeutic parenting. The technique proved counterintuitive and unnatural compared to the way we had been raised. Therapeutic parenting principles are based on the belief that the child sees himself as damaged goods, helpless, and on the verge of falling apart. Recognizing Lee's behavior as a personification of these personal beliefs resonated so loudly with me that I didn't know whether to sob from relief or from utter sadness.

There are times even now when my husband falls back to the bootstrap belief that "Lee should just do it!" Trust me, wishing for implicit and immediate compliance is far easier than remaining calm and showing compassion when all you want to do is have a tantrum of your own over your child balking at taking out the trash or picking up dirty dishes.

As I share how the therapeutic parenting philosophy has positively impacted our family, I want to extend a caveat. I have in no way perfected any parenting plan, as my husband and child will testify, but I do try my best to be consistent in my follow-through and mindful of the underlying reasons for my son's behaviors. Therapeutic parenting, in its purest form, is best done in conjunction with a specialized therapist or counselor who is trained to support the parent. Daniel Hughes's book, *Building the Bonds of Attachment,* tells an exceptional story that shows the practical implementation of therapeutic parenting. However, learning more about it may help inform you about what is best for you.

The principles of therapeutic parenting are based on integrating and assimilating the child's past (most typically done in conjunction with a specialized therapist); parenting with respect and paying special attention to tone of voice, eye contact and physical touch; making decisions that will support success, not failure; recognizing big feelings; and eliminating threats, shaming and punishment.

Therapeutic parenting also emphasizes playfulness, curiosity and empathy. This is known as "dancing with the child's resistance" and it was a wonderful shift in my approach that has helped us tremendously. Take, for example, the need for Lee to interrupt and sabotage my fun. When we were on a family vacation a few years ago, I wanted to go shopping.

He was given the option to go along or stay behind with my husband. He chose to come, knowing he needed new sneakers. When we arrived at the mall, Lee immediately set out to satisfy his shopping list (the new pair of sneakers) and when he was done he insisted we go. Lee is excellent at whining and interrupting any activity that I want to do, so when I started shopping around my interests, he began to whine, glare at me when no one was looking, and do everything he could to get me to give in. The message was "If you loved me, you would make me happy and do what I want."

That's when I realized I could "dance with his resistance." Literally. When he started whining and complaining, I started dancing. I don't mean a little bit, like bouncing up and down subtly while perusing the dress rack. I mean full-on Zumba moves usually reserved for my behind-closed-doors recreation center classes. He was even more mortified when the sales woman came up behind him and said, "Your momma is a sexy dancer!"

The beauty of my public dancing (and occasional singing) is that, for us, it has become an inside joke. It perpetuates a safe relationship while gently reminding Lee that he needs to check his behavior. It is positive, effective and usually evokes eye contact and smiles. I am not out to humiliate him and the moment he stops the behavior that prompted me. I am careful. I stop, too, as a reciprocal sign of respect. I want to preserve that delicate balance between silliness and shame, which can change from day to day. There are times when my silliness lands like a lead balloon, and I try to playfully interact with whatever shows up. Therapeutic parenting is dynamic and creative, and definitely calls on the parent's sensitivity to the child.

If you have hung out with junior high kids lately, you might know that walking this fine line is a daily endeavor. But when you have been trained to watch a child's body language, you will immediately see the impact of your words on him or her. This is true when interacting with anyone, but it is an exceptional rule to remember when parenting.

If you watch your child's body, you'll see that your yelling or shaming (often cloaked as sarcasm or a tone of disdain) will manifest through a pronounced physical reaction. A face or body impacted negatively by words will go limp, as though deflated. It is curious to observe this with a child like yours and mine, because seemingly neutral conversations can have a surprising impact. When this happens Lee shuts down, much like he did when he was first home. He might look like he is listening and engaged, but his body has collapsed and his face is expressionless.

Therapeutic parenting has been very effective for us. It has taught us how to derive meaning from behaviors so that we can act supportively, reminded us that empathy should be a major ingredient in addressing unwanted behaviors and encouraged us to make parenting playful, curious and fun.

One night, curious about Lee's feelings of safety and security, I put him to bed and casually asked if he worried about anything. He said, "Sometimes, when you go out at night, I worry you won't come back." He was nine years old at the time. I knew then that even after years of being with us, he still feared we were temporary. In his mind, even now, his urge to preserve his survival skills (a.k.a. behaviors) is far stronger than his belief that we are a permanent and loving presence that will take care of him forever.

The most profound thing you can do when parenting therapeutically is to be there with your child in their darkest hours, when the hurt and sadness creep in unawares. Our job as parents is not to take away the pain, but to prove that we will be there emotionally, not just physically, no matter how hard it gets. Reassuring them by reflecting their feelings (saying things like, "This is hard. I'm right here,") is the best way to prove your presence over and over again. This is true empathy and it is not always pretty.

Another way we show empathy, as I mentioned before, is through our tone of voice. What we say — a directive, a correction, a request or a feeling — needs to sound sincere. Sarcasm can be a default for many of us (guilty! I think I'm hilarious!), but in some cases it crosses the line. I know I have had to adjust my comments accordingly. If you try, you can probably hear the very thin veil between the sentence "Try again," said with disdain or with compassion and the belief that they can do it better the second time. It's as subtle as the impact of a butterfly wing, but considering the butterfly effect, where one flutter of a wing can start a whole chain of reactions, a change in tone of voice can make a difference too.

It took me years to adapt my parenting to my son's needs. I like to think that, through our efforts, we have come very far. Lee will now sometimes tease me when we hug by putting his arms around my neck and "getting the upper hand" on purpose.

He will also ask me for ridiculous things, like just a soda pop for dinner in the middle of the week. Asking for what he knows is not likely to get a yes entices me to say no, which, in the past would have resulted in me losing my cool or giving him permission to uncork (either of which would have been entertaining for him!). I now know to say, with levity, "Hmmm, sounds like you're setting me up for failure here. You know the rules." For us, that works well and usually results in him smiling and saying, "You got me!"

If I've already answered a question and he begins a political debate on the finer points of a better answer, I say, "You just want to argue!" He laughs and agrees it's true.

There are so many parenting options for us out there. The most intuitive thing for us to do as parents is to seek information that is helpful for us and for our families. Read books, connect with other parents and keep trying. The more you learn, the better you will be at implementing the parenting strategies that resonate with you. Find a combination of philosophies and techniques that let you feel empowered to create a more peaceful home environment. Home can be very hard when you are juggling school demands, emotional burdens and parenting fatigue.

My search for knowledge and help was bringing relief on both the school and home fronts, but there was still another area I was willing to explore in an effort to do all I could for Lee. We were about to plunge in the wild and sometimes crazy world of alternative therapies.

CHAPTER FIVE

Opening to Alternatives

New parenting techniques, counselors and school systems offered much in the way of support for my family and me. Goodness knows, I was open to any and all kinds of interventions, therapies and magic panaceas that promised to alleviate my stress and exhaustion. The funny thing was, while my child operated between typical and not-quite-alarming, my hunt for interventions landed me in a gray area all my own. I was definitely open to both mainstream ideas and just about anything else, short of voodoo, so there was a lot of discerning to be done as I continued my quest for parental perfection.

My definition of acceptable alternative therapies became any offering not typically referred to by educational or medical professionals, but which had documented success and presented no harm if administered, despite the outcome.

At the time I started considering alternative supports, there were scads of articles available on questionable and even dangerous therapies with tragic outcomes, such as a woman who had unexpectedly died in a rebirthing session in Colorado. It was stories like this that gave attachment-specific interventions a bad name and made me hesitate to even consider what else was out there. Today, we are learning so much about brain-based approaches to address anxiety, chronic stress and the healing of early wounds. I suspect this branch of science will only continue to grow.

My hope is that as you read about our experiences, you may slowly open up to the idea that alternative therapies can be a great resource beyond the more traditional techniques available. Most of the supplemental resources I sought were neurologically based, meaning they worked to address early neurological restructuring that we now assume occurs in children who have experienced early adversity and stress. I am also not opposed to working with energy (such as acupuncture and Emotional Freedom Technique). You will know what feels best for you. Whether a technique or therapy is mainstream or not, know that your parenting strength comes from having options and finding support.

I don't know about you, but before deciding what to do, I spent a lot of time desperately trying to name what was happening in our lives. When I taught special education, I knew exactly what to do for each of my students because there were testing protocols that dictated treatment strategies, and diagnostic labels that detailed strengths, weaknesses and effective interventions.

There were no protocols and no labels for my son, but, because of his history, attachment and post-traumatic stress disorders sounded about right. Through research and parental intuition I knew two things: My child overtly exhibited behaviors commensurate with attachment and post-traumatic stress and those behaviors were not severe enough to warrant a psychological evaluation (at least, it has not been necessary so far).

When it came to finding help and interventions, no one could tell me if I was weirdly paranoid, a bad mom or finally on the right track. That's why the Nancy Thomas conference that I attended was so intriguing to me. Her materials arrived in my life at a time when I needed validation about the unique background story and behaviors we were dealing with at home and at school. I knew my son did not play independently, interrupted and demanded constant attention, lied about seemingly innocent things and so on. What I was experiencing with Lee matched a good portion of Ms. Thomas' list of attachment behaviors.

At the conference, I decided to ask her discreetly about self-directed play. I don't remember my exact question, but I remember that her answer was a clear indication that I needed to start parenting with attachment in mind. I can still feel the dread that washed over me. My suspicions had been informally confirmed by an expert.

I scoured information online, like a medical patient with a new diagnosis. Each path led me to new insights, some more sound than others. Wading through information felt like progress at the time, until it became overwhelming.

As Lee's behaviors reached a crescendo, I needed hope, so I set out to find it. I could neither rely on my friends nor on the school for this. They each helped support my quest for peace, but they could not quell the storms that raged on in our home nearly every night, despite my school advocacy and parenting techniques. Those things had helped to get us on the right track, but we were far from having safely arrived.

As my quest continued, I suddenly recalled an earlier search for attachment treatments. At the time, Lee had been only three. My intuition had already guided me to seek help then and I had found something that I resonated with. It had to do with neurological research and it matched up with what I was learning about young brains impacted by early adverse experiences. I had mentally filed it away in case I ever needed it and had considered calling someone about it before, but by the middle of first grade my thoughts had finally become action. Timing is everything. I had reached a personal threshold and I was ready to ask for professional help.

Our Brush with Neurological Reorganization (NR)

This compelling alternative therapy is a neurologically based approach that promised to re-wire the brain after a trauma (emotional or medical, like a stroke) to help mitigate resulting symptoms. It operates on the premise that extreme stress to the brain alters neuropathways, but our malleable brains can be retrained to resume a level of ordinary function. This method was pioneered on stroke victims, but at the time I started using it, it was gaining credence in the international adoption community to assuage the effects of post-traumatic stress.

Our foray into neurological reorganization (NR) started with a trip to Oregon. The phone calls I made to inquire about the program and all the research I had compiled were adding up to hope. I was in need of good news by then.

My husband and I committed to an initial consultation in Portland during spring break. We turned it into a much needed family respite with a side visit to the zoo (where a wily goat ate my husband's road map) and local sightseeing. Everything was unfamiliar, and getting to the office entailed dirt roads, run down tenements, decaying facades and railroad tracks. The whole thing suddenly seemed dodgy. I berated myself for suggesting this endeavor. I now know that all new ventures are a little scary. There is no guarantee that an intervention will work, and the fear of wasting time and money in finding solutions can seem daunting.

Still cautious, we entered an open, sparsely furnished office with massage tables at the far end and a desk near the door. We were introduced to the therapist, a tall, robust woman with a low voice. She invited us into her private meeting room consisting of a table and chairs. I'm sure Dave and I looked scared, or desperate, or both.

Nina, the practitioner, assured us as she closed the door that Lee would be well cared for by the assistant. I was having trouble deciding if this was a bona fide business. I felt a great sense of responsibility at having brought us here.

Once again, I believed our family's well-being rested upon my shoulders and I questioned my good sense.

First, Nina reviewed the extensive questionnaire we'd filled out prior to coming. I had painstakingly completed the paperwork in detail with hopes that this woman could cure our precious little boy. She seemed rather direct at first, and I had a hard time opening up. My husband, true to his nature, didn't say much either.

She asked more questions and explained the origins of NR. She told us that it had originally been used to help stroke victims regain a range of normal functioning by doing what amounted to a brain reset. The premise is that infants, from birth to one year old, go through a developmental sequence made up of sensory, reflex and balance movements designed to develop typical neurology. The idea is that if trauma has affected the neurodevelopment of your child or, for whatever reason, your child has missed a crucial step in the series, the NR process will help to rewire the brain by going back in time, in a way, and re-doing those simple movements. It made sense, especially to me. Because of my background in special education and my avid research up to that point, I had the advantage of speaking her language.

Nina brought Lee into the room and started her baseline neurological assessment. It was not unlike other informal neurological tests that physical therapists might use. Through a series of movements and activities, she could determine where trauma had disrupted his neurodevelopment. By establishing where the glitch started, she could assign infant-like patterns and exercises to rewire the brain from that point.

She showed us several exercises. Some we videotaped to make sure we would remember exactly. Precision and daily follow through were the keys to success. Nina was very clear that this program was not for wimps and wasn't worth it unless we were one hundred percent committed.

The thing about many alternative therapies is they can be grueling, unusual and result-delayed. That means you usually have to give the therapy time to work cumulatively before you might see improvement. If you're me, immediate results are preferable. However, we knew that even if this was a crazy intervention that didn't work, no harm would be done (except to my sanity).

Nina was right. The commitment level of this program was beyond insane. Lee and I would wake up almost an hour earlier each morning to get his army crawls and other mandatory movements done before he left for school. Encouraging him to complete the exercises was far more grueling than doing the protocol itself.

At night, when all three of us were exhausted, we would finish up the day with patterns which required that Lee lay on our dining room table while we positioned his arms and legs and he turned his head in unison with what we were doing. With a choreography rivaling the Shriners at a Fourth of July parade, this activity demanded Lee's full cooperation. Additionally, we had been warned this activity might trigger resistance. It is profoundly impossible to convey the struggle we all endured in getting those crazy patterns done each night. It was tough. But it wasn't all about coaxing Lee to finish grueling drills and then recording his progress.

Making happy neurological connections through eye contact was also a part of the plan, and it brought joy to both Lee and I when he could tolerate it. I would loosely roll him up like a burrito and make silly faces at him as he lay in a blanket. Kisses abounded as did long gazes into one another's eyes like you might do with an infant during feedings. We usually exploded into laughter, dissipating stress and anger.

Before bed we also engaged in sensory activities, like skin surface brushing with a soft brush to evoke calmness, and bone joint stimulation, in which a vibrating massager is used to release cortisol stored in protruding joints like elbows, knees and knuckles. Lee enjoyed these calming activities and they were easy to employ.

In all, executing the NR program added two full hours to our day on top of homework, playtime, sports, mealtime and bedtime. It was a full-time family effort that we completed unequivocally. That included weekends, holidays and birthdays.

I charted everything with the diligence of a laboratory researcher. I followed Lee everywhere with a clipboard, tracking crawls, wiggles and other tasks. I didn't just check off that the activities had been done to the second each day;

I kept track of sleep patterns, general disposition, meltdowns and breakthroughs.

Within a couple of weeks, as Nina had promised, there was one amazing result that fortified our resolve.

This growing boy, who had yet to spend an entire night in his bed, miraculously slept through the night. I still tear up at the immensity of this milestone for us. After just a few days on the NR program, he stayed in his bed from night until morn. The momentous accomplishment of this goal was absolutely staggering. Nina had warned us not to get our hopes up, but she did say that sleeping through the night was often one of the first benefits of NR. It was enough of a carrot for us to keep going. We endured for three long years.

During the time we implemented NR, we traveled twice a year for in-person evaluations, often with incremental results. In doing the program, we didn't even know what we didn't know. For example, NR showed us that Lee did not process hot and cold (which would explain an aversion to winter jackets) and that his eyes weren't tracking correctly (which directly affected his reading).

At the end of our intense run of NR, Lee's visual tracking had improved, his rages had subsided, he was starting to feel cold on occasion, and he slept through the night like a typical kid. We even noticed that his tics could be controlled and he had a higher frustration tolerance. He still had fears and demonstrated hypervigilance, but this felt like progress.

Looking back, my husband and I can't believe we did it. When I remember those intensive days and nights, I am almost brought to tears. Tears because it was so hard on all of us, and tears because our perseverance equaled our fierce love for this little boy from Korea for whom we would literally do anything. It wasn't a cure, but NR took the edge off a lot of things for us.

Not every alternative therapy we tried was a slam-dunk, or even a slow march to victory. We heard about several clients who were supplementing the NR program with cranial sacral work and neurological chiropractic care. Sound scary and bizarre? It can be, especially if you aren't quite sure what it is.

Cranial sacral therapy is relaxing and unassuming. It is a gentle massage technique used to release restrictions in the tissues surrounding the central nervous system. Some believe that this alternative massage therapy can alleviate deep stress and neurological impairment. Lee loved this form of therapy for its calming qualities and stress relief. Whether or not it cured him of emotional baggage is nothing I can quantify with data.

We were referred to another alternative practitioner, a Neurological Chiropractor, by the Neurological Reorganization specialist in order to supplement therapies we were already doing. The neuro-chiropractic adjustments, aimed specifically at improving neurological function, were not different than regular chiropractic adjustments, and Lee agreed that there were benefits. But you'll note I'm not a scientist or an expert. I'm just a mom on an unending quest to help her child.

And that is precisely how I got into one of my more questionable situations. Because alternative therapies are mostly unregulated by state boards, finding reputable care can be tricky. I found out that such clinicians are available in diverse packages. Lacking knowledge of the process, I started to ask around our local California community to see if anyone was familiar with this neurological chiropractic method. Serendipitously (or at least we thought so at the time), a couple we knew had familial connections to someone in the field.

I talked to the office manager (the clinician's wife) at length before signing up for treatments. She was positive, enthusiastic and I knew her relatives. How bad could this be? She suggested that in the next few days I send them an envelope with a lock of my child's hair, a photo from his past in Korea and other random items that seemed to indicate voodoo might actually be part of this process.

You may have noticed the red flags at this point, but my hope disorder kicked in full throttle and I figured this process had to be what others were doing, and surely our friends would not lead us astray.

I dropped off the envelope, as instructed, and was told they needed a few weeks to work with the energy contained in the items. I would be called for an in-depth analysis. I left highly perplexed and intrigued. If nothing else,

I already knew this would make for a fun story at cocktail parties.

Although I was eventually called in for the results, my son was not. His hair was, but his physical being was not. I went to the office alone on a quiet Saturday morning. The clinic was empty except for me, the clinician and his wife. I was led into a back room where apothecary bottles were stored like soldiers at attention on a shelf and an antiquated computer consumed a table.

This behemoth machine purported to register and read the energy of the enveloped trinkets. The reading was alien (that may be literal) and was interpreted by the small, bearded clinician who barely spoke above a whisper. He went through Lee's energetic weaknesses and dietary sensitivities. While it all seemed a little hard to take in, he was accurate when it came to hereditary affectations and symptomology. The accuracies were enough to make me listen to the rest of his spiel.

The treatment was straightforward. He would make special elixirs targeting the first tier of symptoms, and then we would add more as the body worked out certain issues. The visit, with elixirs, was hundreds of dollars, but I kept reminding myself that many others had been happy with this type of intervention. And we knew the practitioners' relatives! I went home, rubbed elixirs on Lee's belly every night, and explained that it would help make him feel relaxed and less stressed at school. I'm pretty sure he thought I was crazy. To his credit, Lee went along with all my wacky ideas.

After the required weeks of topical therapy, we moved into a new round of elixirs. I couldn't tell if anything was working. We were still doing NR, I was trying some new ninja parenting moves, and we were rubbing what looked like water on my kid's belly. It was intervention overload, but we were desperate to help our son find peace and happiness. Quite honestly though, there had been no miracles.

Our final appointment with the soft-spoken, elixir-crafting clinician turned out to be after school and before baseball practice. Unapologetic and abrupt about being almost an hour behind schedule, the clinician's wife sat us down in a waiting room full of patients. She stated curtly that their backed-up schedule was unavoidable due to a dying patient in need of immediate attention. I weighed whether or not to stay. My intuition was to reschedule.

I approached the desk and asked if we could come another time. The attendant looked confused and loudly reiterated what she had stated before: They were attending to a dying man. I was mortified. I sheepishly sat back down, angry now.

She looked at Lee and started talking directly to him.

"Do you want to go to baseball or get better?" she asked him aloud.

Lee looked at me in panic, not quite sure what to do or say.

"What do you want, Lee?" she prodded.

This was getting awkward and I was beginning to fume.

"Get better, I guess," he mumbled.

I was polite but secretly fuming. I told her to cancel our appointment and we left the office. We never returned. I talked to our friends about their relatives and was not surprised to learn that they had only intermittent contact with this couple. Eventually, the couple sold all of their possessions, packed what they had stockpiled into a trailer and were rumored to have moved to an off-the-grid living commune to await worldwide catastrophe.

The experience left a bad taste in my mouth and I berated myself off and on for having wasted the money. In the end, I was able to reconcile that not everything or everybody related to alternative therapies was going to be a radical or even a moderate success. I was also able to check off a therapy I had thought would be worth a try and let it go. It stung for a while, but I still have watery potions I can use to scare off feral neighborhood cats.

Seeking out alternative therapies is like dating. You have to kiss a lot of frogs before you find a good match. Many practitioners are honest, knowledgeable and passionate individuals.

When considering alternative therapies, it's important to keep a few things in mind.

- **Become a detective.** Get to know your child like no one else does and be clear on what you are trying to achieve.

Gather lots of information about the types of challenges you are facing and the options available to address those challenges specifically. The clearer you are about how you want to help your child, the more likely you will be to attract the interventions and therapies that are best suited to your needs.

- **Listen to your intuition.** If you have done your own work and have been able to get clarity around your child's unique needs (and not your wants), then let your intuition guide you. If something feels like a red flag, honor it. No matter your investment, it's always better to walk away mid-stream than to continue funneling your energy into something that isn't working or feels disingenuous. Congratulate yourself on learning a quick lesson and move on. You will know when you find the right people. Trust yourself.

- **Remain open and discerning**. With clarity comes calmness, with calmness comes deeper clarity. It's a cycle that brings you into harmony with yourself and with your child's needs. Be open to hearing suggestions and ideas from those you hold in good esteem. If a suggestion or potential idea doesn't seem right to you at first, step back and do your research. If something seems off to you, then leave it. The best thing about the alternative therapies we tried that didn't work is that none of them had harmful consequences. Most alternative therapies we have sought out are based on Eastern medicine or brain theories that don't require anything but time, money and commitment.

- **Ask a counselor.** Finding the right counselor or therapist for you and your child can be a wonderful support. Having one is paramount to supporting your parental efforts as well as finding alternate resources to fill up your parenting toolbox. Many mental health professionals now have training in alternative therapies to address trauma, like EMDR (Eye Movement Desensitization & Restructuring), which is used to process distressing memories, reduce their long-lasting effects and allow the development of more adaptive coping mechanisms. TRE (Trauma Release Exercises) are exercises that safely activate a natural reflex mechanism of shaking or vibrating that releases stored muscular tension, calming down the nervous system. EFT (Emotional Freedom Technique) combines tapping the energy meridians while voicing positive affirmations, in order to clear the "short-circuit" — the emotional block — from the body's bioenergy system, thus restoring mind/body balance. Whatever feels good to you after considering your options, start there.

Kissing frogs and even finding princes can be arduous. More than once, I have ushered my child to an appointment with hope and curiosity only to wonder how much is too much. Like the number of interventions in a school day, the number of supplemental and alternative supports can feel like being dragged under rather than floating downstream.

I have felt the burden of overload, and it was as heavy as the oversized suitcase I dragged to France last year. Somewhere amid new parenting ninja moves, patterns and potions, I was confronted with the possibility that I was doing this not just to help, but to fix my child. I became more aware of the messages I was sending with my borderline hysterical ways.

"Do you feel like there is always something wrong with you?" I asked Lee once on a drive home from one such appointment.

"All the time," my son stated matter-of-factly.

That's when I realized that maybe, just maybe, there was nothing here for me to fix. I could offer guidance, support and do my best to parent, but I didn't need to fix anything. I was looking at this as a problem to solve rather than a part of a long journey; a journey that was not meant for Lee, but *for me*.

Culture has a way of shaping how we perceive what it means to *do the right thing*. Whether our parameters are imposed by others or imposed by ourselves, sometimes we have to step back from the seduction of trying to make everything better and realize that everything is already okay.

The next alternative intervention I undertook was designed for me. Life coach training gave me the tools and techniques to compassionately observe my situation and recognize my contributions to what was happening. My focus on making everything better — my parenting and the world — was completely reevaluated as I gained the ability to look inside and evaluate what was holding me back.

It was a new way of assimilating Lee's story as part of my own. If you are an adoptive parent or a stepparent, you might think you have this unique child in order to help them, maybe even save them. But what I have learned is that while we are part of their healing journey, we are really in this to heal ourselves. To do that, we must be vigilant about caring for ourselves and compassionately observing our own behavior in an effort to make ourselves, and by extension our children, better.

SECTION THREE

LESSONS ON SELF-CARE

"Yesterday I was clever, so I wanted to change the world. Today I am wise, so I am changing myself."

Rumi

CHAPTER SIX:

Why Manicures and Pedicures Are Not Enough

Living with a child who was dealing with the scary world of early adverse experiences and behaviors created a constant stress in our home. What I never imagined was the way prolonged stress can change the brains of *everyone* in the home. It is not unlike adverse childhood experiences shaping the brain of a developing child. If I think about it simply, I had established my own survival behaviors based on Lee's volatility, much as he had created his own behaviors when he came home to settle in with his third family in less than two years. Connecting the dots with my own affectation was not difficult.

Understanding that a parent could be negatively affected by stress helped me consider a subtle form of what I call post-parenting syndrome (no, it's not a real thing). Our NR practitioner likened it to post-traumatic stress disorder, though making it parallel to a disorder experienced by war heroes and first responders doesn't feel quite right to me. Nevertheless, I started to understand how the implications around living with stress could be true — even for me.

Remember when Lee used to pelt me with his backpack every day in early elementary school? I learned to mentally gear up every single day before I picked him up from school. My body physically tingled and I could feel myself steeling for anything that might come my way. It sounds dramatic, doesn't it? I manage my energy so much better now, but I can remember the day when I first noticed that neurological reorganization was having positive effects on his behavior. I started towards the door to pick Lee up from school and I didn't feel the usual level of dread. A noticeably more relaxed feeling had moved quietly into my soul, though that is not the kind of progress one can easily document.

Unfortunately, I have many stories of how my post-parenting syndrome reared its ugly head. I was often irritable, waiting for the shoe to drop any minute. I sometimes blew up before anything even happened, and the intensity with which I reacted surprised me at times. It was like I was reverting to my own childlike state. I expected things to go badly, slowly etching my own negative core beliefs. I felt more and more out of control. My outbursts and frustrations confirmed that I was indeed neurotic and dramatic — negatively connoted terms my parents had playfully used to describe me when I was a child.

One crucial night when Lee was in third grade, I left our home defeated after a day of difficult events. I taught my evening fitness class, which I thought would help lift me out of the funk. It didn't. I resisted driving home. Instead, I drove to our quaint community theatre, where a Christmas musical was playing. It was a crisp winter night. I had slipped away from home and failed to inform my family of my rogue decision to take in a play — as though I were royalty headed to the Lincoln Center. I was really a sweaty fitness instructor in yoga pants escaping from her mothering failures. I left my phone in the car, paid my admission and sat alone near the stage next to a lovely couple from Minnesota.

I returned late that night to a frantic, worried husband. He knew it had been a particularly rough day, but not knowing where I was or what I was doing for the evening made the situation at home worse. I felt terrible. It was completely unlike me not to check in. My irrational behavior was confirmation that it was time for me to take care of the person in most need of fixing: me.

I searched for and found a counselor. She was 45 minutes away, had also adopted and raised two children with attachment issues, and was highly attuned to the pitfalls of a perfectionist mom trying to control a child with his own ideas about the world. She offered solid parenting advice while focusing on my anxiety, using mainstream techniques peppered with esoteric audio files whose stories were magical metaphors for healing. I loved her.

Half the battle was finding an empathetic ear and calming ideas and strategies for personal empowerment. The other half of my personal battle was centering myself. I needed to combat the doubt and frustration I was feeling by creating and working towards a more positive vision for myself and my family. That meant taking better care of me — and I don't just mean massages and manicures.

Calgon commercials have long promised to "take me away" (and I don't mean by a shady character in a windowless van), and I needed more of that. Time away from perpetually challenging parenting was precious and necessary. Luckily, I had a truly supportive husband and I had already released myself from any guilt over taking a girl's weekend away. Hey, when parenting is tough, you feel like you've earned a break!

But even when I gave myself permission to take a spa weekend, the countdown to the inevitable Sunday night re-entry started the minute my friends and I drove away from home and went through the local gourmet coffee shop for the fancy breakfast sandwiches our children would have hated. From the first sip of caramel macchiato, I would spend the whole weekend trying to slow the hands of time just as futilely as I tried to control the homework habits of my teenager.

The act of pampering myself with quick getaways, pedicures and massages seemed too fleeting. They were momentary releases from the grip of what I defined as a harsh reality. If I were running a marathon, that kind of pampering would be the part where I paused to walk or take a drink, just long enough to restore resolve and get me across the finish line. Pampering allowed me to breathe, regroup and gain the strength to face one more argument, tame one more outburst, or make one more family meal. It was a much-needed break in the marathon of motherhood, but, while those indulgences were temporarily delightful, their effects remained far too short-lived.

What I eventually discovered was true self-care. Acts of real self-care penetrate far deeper than the superficial reprieve of pampering. True self-care practices helped create a more empowered constitution and taught me how to release parental suffering, no matter the momentary circumstance. I have come a long way since that wintry night at the community theatre.

After regularly engaging in self-care techniques, I have far fewer outbursts, am able to remain calm in most circumstances, and quickly notice when I'm not at my best. Isn't it ironic that these are the very behaviors I have wanted to improve in my son? By changing my way of being, my family has responded, too. It wasn't easy, but as sung in the musical *Wicked*, *"I have been changed for good."*

My favorite methods of self-care are breathing, yoga, meditation, being in nature and mindfulness. I want to share them with you as part of this parenting memoir in the hope that you will also find them useful.

Breathing sounds pretty straightforward, but it's a good thing breathing is an unconscious biological response or I'd probably forget to do it. Most often, we breathe shallowly, tensing our bodies and holding stress in our muscles. By taking one to three deep breaths when we feel tense, we relax and counteract the fight, flight or freeze mechanism. (Which may or may not be useful when attacked by a child Nerf sniper in your own home. Yes, that has happened to me.) A great way to understand the concept of relaxation through breathing is yoga.

Yoga comes in many forms. There is no need to put your feet behind your head in an advanced class, bake yourself from the inside out in hot yoga or feel weird chanting and moaning in Sanskrit. Honestly, I used to avoid yoga like a mom with a toddler avoids the candy aisle. It seemed impossible to quiet my mind and be still. I had secret visions of getting up and running over my yoga neighbor on the next mat over, for the entertainment. And the pretzel poses? I don't think so!

Who knew this was the perfect attitude for beginning a yoga practice? The point of yoga is not to be still and flexible on the first try. It's a way to *learn* and *practice* those things. Yoga has many documented benefits, including stress reduction, increased flexibility and pain reduction, among many others. It also keeps me calm when parenting, negotiating with my spouse and dealing with snarled traffic.

Meditation is yoga's calming companion, but it is not napping (although there are benefits to that, too!). Being in a quiet, reflective state without distraction can actually change our brains for the better (our brains are so malleable). Meditation is not about learning to control your thoughts; it's about learning how not to let them control you! Start with three minutes — even if you have to lock yourself in the bathroom. I have done that, and though I still struggle to make meditation part of my regular day, I notice a huge difference when I fit it into my schedule. It's similar to spending quiet time in the morning and setting an intention for the day. It allows me to focus and create the best in every moment. Meditation's effects are subtle and long-lasting.

One of my favorite meditations for tough situations is something I learned from Martha Beck, a renowned author and my life coach training mentor. This unique type of meditation, which she called Quantum Meditation, allows us to mentally "time travel" and be there in the past for someone (including our younger selves) as we are now. For example, I have meditated on the moment my son was relinquished in Korea. I imagine the room, his birth mother, her mother and the social worker. I imagine Lee on his birth mother's lap, and then her finally having to go. I'm sure Lee reached for her as she closed the door, and wailed in the aftermath as the social worker held him. I know, because we met with his social worker when she was in Denver mere months after his arrival. She was overcome when she saw Lee again, weeping openly and hugging him tightly.

I have imagined that scene in my mind and envisioned myself as a calm bystander in that room, telling Lee that all will be well, assuring him until his intense reaction subsides. I create a calm re-write of the story, with loving outcomes and the best intentions to be the future mother he needs and deserves.

I have also meditated this way by conjuring a calm version of myself appearing in my mind when I am highly upset or sad. How weird is that?! In my mind's eye, this calmer version of me reminds me that fretting and worrying are only temporary, that whatever is happening will work out. It is such a lovely way to connect with a peaceful, trusting part of myself. That's what meditation teaches us to do — trust and be still.

Being in nature is soothing for the soul and requires nothing but breathing the air around you and taking in the vast miracle that everything is alive. Hanging out with flora and fauna can reduce depression, anxiety and general malaise. I think the impact of nature is highly underrated.

You can read about the restorative qualities of nature on the Internet or in most journals. Research has proven over and over that time outdoors has positive physiological and psychological effects — and in our family there is no better proof than a relaxed, engaged and laughing child.

We have conducted our own informal family research and I can attest to the improved attitudes of everyone when we stash our phones and play outdoors beneath the clouds, sun and stars. At the end of any outdoor activity, we typically enjoy one another more and are better conversationalists.

Nature helps us connect us with loved ones. On a recent trip to Arizona, I was reminded of just how powerful family connection can be. We spent much time outside, including bouncing around mightily along dry creek beds in a jeep, soaking up amazing views. Jovially thrown about the rented vehicle, I played up my fear of toppling over (and peeing my pants) during the 4x4 experience. The next day, I was legitimately apprehensive when we saddled onto ATVs and had to steer our own motorized vehicles over protruding rocks and deep ruts. My son ridiculed my sloth-like speed.

There is no better sound than a giggling, awed teenager seeing his controlled, nagging mom lose her mind around motor vehicles, red dust and wildly uneven ground. They say laughter is the best medicine. I know it was soulful medicine to laugh with my kid like that. Connecting in the wilds of the red desert without electronics was effortless.

The ultimate feeling of connectedness and expansiveness occurred for us at the Grand Canyon, when we walked for miles along the South Rim. There is no way to feel mightier than nature in those moments. I'm not a fan of heights, and my personal limitations were apparent, while my son and husband found every scenic outcrop along the way, standing toe to toe with nature's imposing depth. On a particularly daunting hike down into the canyon, the sheer drop-offs had me clinging for life and insisting my family go on while I tried to prevent a paralyzing panic attack. Once again, mom failed epically, to the delight of her kid. Lee hiked fearlessly down the narrow, harrowing path and back up without complaint. He was proud of his efforts. Such moments are brought to us by the power of nature.

Being in nature reminds family members to respect, encourage and look out for one another, which makes the benefits profound. There is a relaxation and release that helps to make dinnertime conversation after such adventures interactive and fun, and ignites a desire to stay connected through games and dialogue, rather than turning on the television. There is an innate feeling of connectedness and cooperation generated that prompts us to be kind and inclusive. Nature is fuel for our families and fuel for our souls.

Next time you're out in nature, notice more than the beautiful scenery and fresh air. Notice how different you feel and how connected you are to your family and friends.

Mindfulness can become a way of life. Recently, I completed training as a community educator of Mindfulness Based Stress Reduction (MBSR). It entailed a regular yoga practice, sessions of guided meditation, classwork and a promise to teach others. At the heart of mindfulness is a desire to train ourselves to pause in that millisecond between reaction and conscious action. That millisecond can mean the difference between lashing out and responding with purpose. Without mindfulness we interact with the world this way:

Circumstance –> Thought –> Reaction

With mindfulness we interact this way:

Circumstance –> Thought –> Awareness –> Response

Without awareness of how we are feeling and reacting, we are likely to respond to a situation based on our thoughts (which are created through personal experience, previous learning and feeling). This results in a spontaneous retort we think is beyond our control and appears to be based on the circumstance. I have learned that it is far too easy to make a situation or another person's behavior the excuse for my reactions. Mindfulness allows me to recognize my thoughts as the fickle beings they are and instead to create a response based on my values and who I choose to be.

Let me give you an example based on my favorite subject — homework. My experience and formula for school success is based on my belief that I am a very good student. Therefore, the way I do things in a school situation is, to me, effective and right. I'm highly visual, I like writing and I thrive in typical classrooms because they cater to my kind of learning. I like organizing my materials, writing to-do lists and completing assignments. These seem like fairly easy tasks to accomplish. My son, on the other hand, finds my winning combination repulsive and nearly impossible to carry out on a regular basis. He finds organization and assigned tasks overrated. Just look at his room! It should probably be condemned by a health agency.

When he was off to junior high, I acted like most parents. I worried about how he would fit in, how the teachers would treat him and how he would achieve academically. In anticipation of schoolwork being harder (yes, I had already determined this), I noticed myself gearing up for the battle. I sat Lee down and suggested we make a pre-plan for school success. You might imagine I had a few ideas. I may even have been more bossy and anxious than suggestive and mindful.

Lee was not receptive to my ingenious ideas (even though I had teaching credentials and insider information). He listened to my rambling suggestions and let me create all kinds of charting systems intended to keep him (or was that me?) on track. Within two weeks of school starting we were locked in a constant after-school battle threatening to drive us both mad. Did I feel like parenting was hard?

Yes, I knew we would need a true miracle, or at least a Dr. Phil intervention, to get through junior high.

I moped around, nagging Lee like a possessed golden retriever to finish his homework. I put binders teeming with papers in order at the end of each day and I harped on him to do his chores. In an obviously futile effort, I insisted on going through this ritual every night. Other parents did it and it worked for them, right? My job was to raise a responsible, self-motivated, delightful individual. I could not give in. I would not relinquish my responsibility to bring this young man into adulthood on a white stallion. I would harp on him until he magically decided that my ways were nothing short of nirvana designed to change him into an over-achiever, while other parents lauded his talented mother. I was definitely putting my expectations and ideas before our relationship.

None of what I wanted to happen happened. Not even a little bit. In fact, what happened was I got so frustrated and discouraged by the lack of civility between us that I started to question my parenting. I had no idea what to do, which is a scary place to be when you have a kiddo with a tendency to spiral into failing grades and disengage faster than you can set off a warning flare.

My training in Mindfulness Based Stress Reduction finally kicked in and I stepped away from the problem. I ditched the charts, the nagging and the need for his room to clean itself. I allowed myself to be comfortable with not knowing the answer immediately. Calmly pulling back the lens on our problem, I invited clarity into my conundrum. There is perspective lost when we get right in there and parent full-throttle, which usually chokes the life out of our kids. I didn't need to react to what I considered a daily failure of undone work and less-than-pristine binders.

I have noticed that in times of not-knowing, I can still breathe. It is not my job to micromanage. Giving myself permission to *not know* what comes next in the parenting plan allows me to simply watch, to be a compassionate observer of my child, who is himself learning. That alone can feel like relief. When I continue to force what I know is not working, like lists and charts, I am too wrapped up in disappointment and frustration to stop and consider what other methods might be worth a try. Stepping back from a situation gives me time to catch my breath and consider alternatives. Not only am I relieved, but so is my child.

When I release the need to do it My Way, something happens. The channels of ingenuity and creativity allow new ideas. It reminds me of the book *Of Mice and Men* by John Steinbeck. I was always intrigued by Lenny, the cognitively simple friend of George, who would begin petting innocent, small animals with a genuine tenderness. His enthusiasm for petting the soft animals grew until he literally choked the life out of them. He never meant to harm them, but he could not control his ever tightening grasp.

We can have the same tendencies when it comes to our children. We love them so much and want to protect them from failure, ridicule or even bad grades. We want to be sure their behavior reflects their best selves so as not to cast a negative or judgmental shadow upon our good name. If we just micromanage every second, moment, day, then all will be well.

That's the way I felt when I created my start-of-school charting systems and to-do lists. In the spirit of helping Lee succeed, I was basically suffocating him with a regimen so dictatorial and against his nature that failure was the only option. After what I knew was an exhausting day for him, I met him at the door with a list of chores, inspections and expectations. I combed through every binder, all of which were hemorrhaging crumpled college-ruled paper. He felt absolutely no compulsion to organize or even manage his binders of ill repute. He still doesn't.

Beyond the binders, he would balk at reading for the required twenty minutes a day and never quite get to the dishes. His daily planner, the required school and home go-between tool, was basically a piece of home décor on permanent display as part of our coffee table arrangement. I followed him around at the end of each day, pointing out every incomplete item. It was grueling for me, debasing for him.

When I finally got tired enough of criticizing his every move, I surrendered. After weeks of arguing and nagging, I finally understood that I didn't have to keep charts, lists and tallies. I threw them all away. It felt like a weight had been physically lifted. Don't get me wrong, I was still frustrated and grasping at ideas to support him, but I didn't have to spend energy keeping track of what I already knew he wasn't doing. I let it marinate. He knew what he needed to do, so I left it alone for the time being and praised what he did, which was pretty much the basics of what needed to be done.

In the end, I allowed the teachers, all of them concerned and helpful, to do their jobs. The school had so many checks and balances that Lee didn't need me to interfere with their promise to help him succeed. All I did was keep in touch with his teachers, promise to help when they needed me, and collaborate when it was warranted. I let him figure out how to do it his way and helped when I was asked to.

Mindfulness, with practice, can lead to a new, more compassionate way of looking at the world and your child. When I was mindful, it brought attention to how much my fears perpetuated my own controlling behaviors, which ultimately clashed with Lee's own need for control. By understanding the difference between my problems and his I have come to know a greater peace.

But I am no monk on a mountaintop. (There is a reason most enlightened people don't have kids!) Rest assured, there are still days I fall short of my best, but mindfulness allows an awareness that my failings are temporary and typically a sign that self-care needs to be a priority or that I need to address something in my life that is creating stress. By practicing self-care, I have empowered myself to be adaptable in all circumstances. Kind of like a thought ninja.

Becoming a thought ninja is a deeper way of exploring and implementing mindfulness. It allows us to consider that our thoughts and experiences may perpetuate some of our suffering. Yes, parenting a child with early adverse experiences is exhausting and stressful, but working through some of our own negative thought patterns can ease the tension, even if it does require work and lots of practice.

CHAPTER SEVEN

Becoming a Thought Ninja

As you already know, there is an art to parenting a child who has both the traits of a typical kid and the subtleties of a child with attachment disorders. On the one hand, I could evaluate everything my son does through the jaded lens of exceptionality, attributing all his quirks to his early plight. Or I could turn that lens into rose-colored glasses and choose to see the developmentally typical behavior as a sign that all is fine, denying him the continued support he truly needs. That is the thin line we walk every day. We decide whether to respond to the needs of our child as a savior (insert orchestral music here) or as a supportive, knowledgeable guide. These days, I am beginning to identify far more with the latter than the former, but it's taken some effort on my part to move into a space where there is not just hope, but empowerment and optimism.

Malcolm Gladwell's book *David and Goliath: Underdogs, Misfits, and the Art of Battling Giants* makes the compelling argument that most successful people in the world have thrived despite, or potentially because of, adversity. I love this idea. When I discovered it, I stopped telling myself that Lee's early childhood experiences created limits and started to look at his personality traits and experiences as rich soil for future success. Lee's past could potentially be limiting, but both of us had a lot to gain by viewing his experiences as a source of strength and an indicator of his resilience. The opportunities for him were limitless if I could help him appreciate and accept that what seemed like weaknesses might just as easily be seen as strengths.

I began to ponder all of the qualities that before had seemed annoying, difficult and even frustrating to me as his parent. Based on Gladwell's assertion that adversity can translate into success, I decided to see Lee's attributes as strengths. Perhaps I was the only parent too myopic and caught up in my own worry frenzy to see the obvious. When I flipped my thinking about Lee's and my daily struggles, I realized that my child is intuitive, aware, sensitive, compassionate, persistent, resilient, funny, forgiving, brave, thoughtful, athletic, law-abiding, considerate, resourceful and stronger than I thought. All of a sudden, his crazy arguing sounded rather like that of a lawyer, a politician or a salesman. His school reports indicate a continuously positive attitude, despite the constant barrage of negative academic feedback. His perseverance truly astounds me. If I had been faced with his circumstances, I would have given up long ago, or at least become more resigned than he is. Every day, he continues to give it his best shot. There will be room in this world for him if I can remember to see his challenges as the gifts they are in honing resiliency.

For me, the key to truly reconciling and restructuring my old thought patterns was to become a thought ninja. How does one become a thought ninja? Well, it's highly classified information on the mommy circuit, but I'm willing to tell you if you promise not to just slap a smile on your face and pretend that your pet unicorn is pooping gold. It's easy to say you're serene and comfortable with imperfection, even if that's only an aspiration most of the time. Being a thought ninja is hard work. You have to become aware of your own triggers, and be willing to see them differently, if even for a millisecond.

Pretend you are in a fitness class, like Zumba, where you totally know the choreography to your favorite song inside and out. You can sing, dance and make funny faces all you want because your body automatically knows when to jive, body bump and shimmy. After tons of repetition in the classes, your brain has built a pathway for doing those steps and they are easy now that you've had experience. Now, pretend a new instructor comes in and uses the same song but different choreography. It feels weird, confusing and potentially irritating. You start to body bump when she starts to shimmy, you feel awkward in general and you just want to go back to what you know. That can be what it feels like to change behavior in the face of a personal trigger.

The best way I have found to hone my ninja skills is with a combination of mindfulness and what I call "power questions." Mindful awareness, which I touched on in the previous chapter about self-care, is the ability to intercept a thought: catching a reaction, questioning it and diffusing it in an effort to give a more thoughtful, meaningful response. Let me give you an example from my real life that will demonstrate my infinite wisdom — and my (often) poor execution.

As you know, yoga is high on my self-care list. After years of regular practice, I feel a deeper connection to my self and a genuine detachment from comparing myself to other yogis in the class. It has taken me years to internalize the mantra "no judgement and no competition" that our teacher recites regularly to remind us to stay on our own mats (that's yoga-speak for "mind your own business"). But just when I think I have mastered my inner child, she shows up unexpectedly, reminding me that personal growth is always evolving.

In one particular class, a young, male student who was new to the class made every pose we did seem easy. He wrapped himself into geometric shapes accomplished only by those seemingly without connective tissue. The teacher was impressed and used him as the model for a particular yoga sequence. Most of the class attempted the basic concepts of the sequence. I pushed myself into muscle spasms to go pose for pose with young yogi man. On the final posture that challenged us to balance only on our hands, I hoisted myself into the precarious pose for a full second before teetering onto my face.

Here's the good news. As I started to compete, I mindfully observed my reaction to this new student and his physical abilities. I noticed myself preening for the attention of the instructor and wanting to shout, "Hey, I can do that too! Look at me!" I recognized a little girl, the oldest of five, wanting to be acknowledged for her own accomplishments. My revelation was so helpful. I was able to come back to my mat and do what felt best for me. It wasn't easy and I still probably stepped up my yoga game unnecessarily. My point is about mindfulness and awareness. Without them, we don't even know what we don't know about ourselves.

Power questions are really a way of noticing our thoughts, as I did in yoga class that day, with the goal of releasing the feelings and judgments that cause suffering. I want to share some questions that I use on myself when I become aware of those anxious, sad or helpless mother feelings.

Will this matter in five years?

There isn't much on a daily basis that is going to matter in five years. If it will, then you have my permission to panic. As you know, grades and school are important to me. With only weeks left in Lee's seventh grade year, I walked smack into my son's grades lying out on the counter. I don't have to tell you it looked bad. It looked like he was about to fail a class despite having hung in there all year! Apparently, he had not yet handed in assignments for the final chapter. I felt the rise of my inner perfectionist gripping my insides and wanted to begin an immediate lecture on the finer points of responsibility, perseverance and a job well done. That's when I went into thought ninja mode and considered something more true and useful.

My child learns and operates differently in school than I ever did. Because he has had to conform to the system laid out for him, he takes full advantage of the current you-can-hand-in-assignments-anytime-for-partial-credit rule. Not every school operates this way, but his does. Lee's grades often look sketchy, but when he gets behind, the school offers support and makes sure he gets everything completed and turned in. Students are also allowed to retake tests, and Lee admits they're easier for him on the second try. I'm not suggesting that kids not do their work, but I have known Lee long enough to appreciate his understanding of the system.

The bottom line is, even if he failed the class, it would not have curtailed his academic career. My seventh-grade achievements are forgotten. My grades in junior high have had no bearing on my life since then. Some of what happens in the course of my son's educational career is his business. I reminded myself that certain experiences will speak far more loudly than my incessant lecturing.

Recognizing his characteristics as what they are challenges me to consider that he may just know what he is doing. Allowing him to create solutions while I quietly monitor and help from the sidelines (as an offer and not a directive) has proven so much more effective than my loud diatribes and disapproving looks. It is no easy task to accept that your child may simply operate differently than you do, and it has taken me many attempts in the face of challenges to get here, but I can now accept that my child's way of dealing with a situation is not mine. I'm still close by to make sure he won't spiral into an impossible situation that he can't climb out of. It is a fine balance, requiring intuition and trust that I'll know when to step in if needed.

How can I make this easy?

This is one of my favorite questions because it usually comes to me when I am doing a thousand things at once and fighting overwhelm. In those moments, I can get snippy and grouchy, which never helps when you're the parent. Have you ever noticed how when you seem to be short on coping skills your kids can smell that like a fox can smell a chicken coop? My son usually ramps up his own behavior in relation to mine. I have learned that when I become overwhelmed, there are easy solutions to relieve the perceived pressure. A solution could be as easy as substituting a rare freezer meal for a home-cooked one at the last minute or hiring out house cleaning when your in-laws are coming and you have too many other things to do. Those small tasks that lead to hours of juggling your child's behavioral challenges and the need for your responsiveness can be exhausting. I've learned to let go of a lot and make my life as easy as I can when it counts.

Since I live with a skilled negotiator who loves to argue, one way I've made things easy for myself is to embrace the voice in my head that says, "Stop talking." Not responding when a conversation has turned the corner into an argument has been pure gold. It shuts down opportunities to escalate the situation and keeps in check my need to lecture. It also preserves everyone's dignity. Is it easy? No — I have cut myself off mid-speech. But my continuous efforts have definitely paid off.

How is this perfect right now?

This question prompts me to shift my thinking quickly in tough situations, especially as a parent. By asking how my situation is perfect right now, I remember to open up to the possibilities of why something is happening.

I find this particularly compelling when I get frustrated in traffic because the person ahead of me is testing the physics of inertia and I have to be somewhere. If I ask myself how this is perfect right now, I tell myself that I may be stuck behind a slower person because it helps me follow the speed limit. More than once I've passed a police car while giving grateful thanks for having been stuck behind a slow person. I also remember that I am sometimes that slow person with nowhere to be, just enjoying where I am going, completely oblivious to the guy behind me who may be late. See how that works? We are at times the thing we despise. One of my favorite Buddhist quotes offers an enlightening and gentle perspective: "You are not stuck in traffic; you are the traffic."

This question can also help me combat perfectionistic tendencies. If my child is failing, I know it's perfect because it's an opportunity for him to make his own way and find his own solutions to life's problems. If Lee and I are having a rough patch with lots of disharmony, it is perfect because it invites me to step back and explore the basis of why we are discordant with one another. This question also works on the big decisions that may seem permanent, like when my siblings and I helped my mom spread my dad's cremains on his favorite golf course. He had passed away suddenly, but had also said for years that there was a specific golf course hole on which he wanted to posthumously reside. The problem was he had mentioned two different holes to two different family members! It could have been the cause for a paralyzing debate, but our mantra on the days we were together for his funeral was: "This is perfect." Whether it was the setup of the church or what we did or didn't do in our time of grief, it was all perfect. I know it can sound trite in a very emotional situation, but there was something about being able to scatter my dad's cremains while knowing that wherever they ended up would be perfect, despite our uncertainty about his specific wishes.

This question is the ultimate reminder to accept what is happening. If I can't change it, acceptance is my only option. I accept by looking at the problem through a different lens and creating alternate truths that ease my frustration or suffering. Do you know how you can tell that something is perfect? Because it's what's happening.

Is it time to get back to basics?

We occasionally like getting back to basics around our house because it resets both Lee and me. You already know

Lee is as persistent as a politician and is highly gifted in understanding systems, enabling him to perform the least amount of work necessary to fulfill said system's requirements (like taking out the trash or doing dishes). It's quite impressive. He can also demonstrate varying thresholds for frustration (so can I). To counter bouts of high irritability or stress, I intermittently implement my signature Back to Basics Boot Camp, intended to inspire more gentle and ethical aspirations. This involves an elaborate, famous charting system, whereby Lee earns luxuries like rides to school (we have a bus that stops right outside our door), electronics, and desserts by adhering to behaviors with a heavy emphasis on calm and cooperation.

After a few days of limited electronics, television shows and high-sugar snacks, there is a distinct reboot of his behavior, and he becomes more pleasant and easygoing. It's my way of teaching him self-care. After a break from electronics and unhealthy eating, we talk about how he feels. Even he concedes that he feels like a better, calmer person when some stimuli are limited, even if temporarily.

How can I take care of myself?

This is a double entendre question. When things start to deteriorate for me, I first ask myself this question so I'm reminded to stay in my own business from the outset. It reins me in when I start meddling in my son's problems too much, and helps me remember that I have to take care of my own emotional stuff first. That makes me more effective as a parent.

As soon as I feel myself being drawn into anger, I take a deep breath and consider what is really happening. Often, I will realize it's part of the pattern where I am judging my son's behavior against my lofty expectations, or perhaps I am just tired. I am most often argumentative when something unrelated to my child is bothering me and he then becomes the perfect outlet for my need to vent. Funny how that works.

Secondly, if I am getting frazzled or tired from too many nights without quality sleep, I ask myself what would feel like self-care. Can I fit in a nap? Can I meditate or make it to yoga today? Do I just need some quiet time without distractions? Will I send regrets to a meeting that feels like too much today? I am getting so very good at not only identifying my needs, but also following through and actually providing myself with what I need. I have a supportive husband, who is exceptional at doing everything in his power to give me quiet time or to help me get to yoga. In most of my years as a stay-at-home mom I only taught my family how to need me. Now I teach them to count on me when they need it and to support me in my endeavors, too. Our family is a symbiotic triad, not a one-woman show, even if moms do have a special way of setting the climate in a family.

I don't pretend to be the best thought ninja in the world, but I know that thinking about situations differently has led me to an acceptance of my son and to a deeper connection with him. I hope it's because I have changed and that might provide the smallest bit of inspiration for him to do the same. He's a teenager, so I'm planting seeds with hope of future blossoms.

While mindfulness and thought-questioning may sound easy, it's not. I have been just as volatile as my child at times, with great regret. During Lee's third-grade year, I didn't think I would make it, but I was willing to keep working with the tools I learned in an effort to be more thoughtful. Most recently, on a much-needed spa weekend, I noticed that I had come a long way from the anxious mom I once was.

The weekend getaway started with a glassblowing class. For the record, glassblowing is not as easy as it looks, and the constant danger of disfiguring yourself or others with third-degree burns is imminent and terrifying. The oven housing the liquid glass is heated to 2100 degrees. Looking into it is like looking into the depths of hell — literally. It's so hot that your brain freaks out and wants to run away instead of calmly gather the raw material for an art project. Glassblowing, like most crafts, is not in my wheelhouse. If you know me, you know that crafting is the antithesis of my general existence. But I do love to try new things.

Our instructor, Dan (let's call him the Willie Nelson of glassblowers), was a complete delight, both reassuring and enthusiastic about teaching this newcomer. He helped me craft a paperweight by standing next to me, giving step-by-step instructions and encouragement. Things could get ugly fast and Dan was right there to avoid disaster. Although I managed not to injure myself, my circular paperweight began to look more oblong than round, and it sustained a permanent scar when I failed to follow the turn-at-all-times rule that helps glassblowers create a smooth, circular shape.

Leaving the studio that day, I was drawn to a beautifully colored vase Dan had for sale. I just knew I had to have it, so I bought it and stuck it in the seat pocket of my car, where it stayed for the entire weekend. The beautiful green vase evoked warm memories and I couldn't wait to put it somewhere special in my house.

Arriving home from the exhilarating but tiring weekend, I unpacked my things from the vehicle and just as I was about to grab the glass vase, it hopped out of the car and onto the asphalt, shattering everywhere. I was devastated. I stared at the shards and brought my hands dramatically to my face. I couldn't believe I had done that! I was overwhelmed with sudden sadness. It was a curious and intense response to a broken piece of glass. Honoring my feelings, I went inside quietly and sunk into a bath.

But in the morning, I asked myself, "How is this perfect right now?" I was able to come up with three truths that helped reduce my disappointment.

First, my experience was amazing! I had photos, memories and a great story to tell. The broken vase had nothing to do with my warm memories of the weekend.

Second, I had ultimately purchased the vase to support the artist. Just because it no longer existed for me, my support endured. He still had my payment.

Finally, I had learned that day during our session that Dan had lost a child to leukemia. I had lost a vase, but he had lost a daughter. I had come out pretty well if all I had to do was sweep shards into the garbage.

That perfectly formed vase was fleeting and had been produced by the master. I was left with an imperfect, oblong-shaped paperweight that I had made myself. It was a wonderful metaphor reminding me that I am flawed and imperfect. So is my child. We are both muddling through our circumstances together, and while our efforts may seem inadequate in comparison to others, our accomplishments and our failures have crafted a very solid, beautiful story.

I love my glassblowing story because it illustrates how far I have come and it demonstrates the thought ninja process so beautifully. It is the process I use with my son, the one I use for my life. I knew that a broken vase wouldn't matter in five years; I took care of myself when I was still feeling the disappointment by soaking in a bath; when I was ready, I challenged myself to find a better way of thinking.

But I want to be really clear about this so you don't go forth and think a herd of magical unicorns has converged on your lawn. They haven't. They won't. This is not a formula to make you a permanently optimistic person or to lull yourself into passively accepting the things that can, in fact, be changed. I often find that our culture is bent on ushering us as quickly as possible through life's inevitable rough patches under the guise of "positive thinking." As though it's not okay to feel the real feelings that disappointment and struggle can bring. Being a thought ninja is not that. Saying you are fine, and ignoring real feelings when life gets hard for you or your child, can almost seem dismissive. If life hands you lemons, you don't have to make lemonade right away. Parenting a child with early adverse experiences is hard and exhausting. Trust me, sometimes you just need to let a lemon be a lemon. That's when honoring your need for pampering and self-care can help you process and work through the deep feelings.

Processing and working through deep, real feelings are just as important as using your ninja moves to examine your thoughts. When we examine a thought with active questioning, we are reminding ourselves that creating a negative story can create undue suffering. But there are times that it is appropriate to excavate and feel your own big feelings; if it results in your own tantrum involving screaming into pillows or having a good cry, so much the better.

Part of being the parent of a child with early adverse experiences means acknowledging that you may feel isolated, set apart and desperate. It can mean feeling frustration, anger and complete exhaustion at the prospect of continually managing big feelings, your own and your child's. I have dealt with many tough feelings before emerging to where I find myself now. I call those low moments when I have felt the most desperate and hopeless "quiet seasons."

Quiet seasons can descend upon you like a shadow creeping in the night or as forcefully as a meteor. They will take your breath away, leave you numb and alter your perception.

They can envelop and suffocate you until the only thing left to do is quietly sit in the darkness wondering what has happened and how you will ever get away. The darkness will be terrifying, but you will never outrun it. The only escape is to go through it blindly, relying on your senses until slivers of light begin to illuminate a new path.

What happens during a quiet season is not unlike what happens in winter. There is a cold barrenness that blankets the spirit and inspires hidden growth deep inside, whether we are ready or not. It seems to rob us of beauty, warmth and inspiration, but in that stark latency are the subtle beginnings of profound transformation. Slowly, we begin to shed what is no longer needed and embrace new strengths and realizations.

I learned the most during a very quiet season that started when my father unexpectedly died two days before my forty-fourth birthday. It was also the day of my mother's last cancer treatment, a week out from my brother's stay in ICU from sepsis, and the day before I was to return to California and pack up our family for a move back to Wyoming. It was an emotional avalanche so powerful that resistance was futile. As I wandered through airports, navigated the streets of my old town, or walked out of a room, I sensed I was leaving something behind. It was irrational, but so compelling that leaving my car, my home, or a hotel room required consulting a comprehensive checklist rivaling that of a NASA space shuttle launch. Every day, every moment, something was just missing.

When the movers arrived at my soon-to-be-former house, they ruthlessly started packing up everything I owned. There was no ceremony, no reverence, and no sympathy. Like packing tape being ripped away, leaving me raw, I felt exposed and wounded. Without a word, I succumbed to the dragon of despair at three o'clock that afternoon. I slithered carefully to my son's former room and cocooned myself under his comforter, hoping to find asylum.

In that cocoon, I thought of all the moments within those four walls when I had held my boy as he wailed and mined his own bottomless pit of despair. I remembered the tender moments he finally looked into my eyes and peppered me with questions about his Korean mother, and the funny rituals like rubbing watery elixirs on his belly. Somehow, losing a parent and the comforts of what I knew as home felt like gazing into a crystal ball. I was seeing into Lee's toddlerhood, but from my perspective as an adult. I had some sense of the deep, paralyzing grief my little boy must have felt a decade before in a small room at a Korean adoption agency. That kind of loss changes you. His need for emotional purges, his dysregulation with the ordinary and his weariness for life were understandable. It is hard to process deep feelings. It takes a long time; even as an adult with a developed brain, it was pretty mind-numbing. As the cacophony of the movers went on around me, I eventually fell asleep.

From an observer's perspective, it may have looked like a peaceful slumber. But like a butterfly metamorphosing, there was action and healing in my quietude. What seemed like rest was really healing. As our bodies beckon for us to be still or react to feelings (for me, the reaction is always sleeping), so our strength and spirit regenerate. I realized intuitively that it was wise to honor my body's weary inclinations for sleep, anger, frustration, for giving up. All those feelings would pass, and a butterfly would eventually emerge.

My personal need for rest and hibernation during this recent quiet season ebbed and flowed through the packing, the funeral and the move. When I arrived for good on the doorstep of our new home in Wyoming, the snow-laden city mirrored my wintery, frozen soul. Just like the arrival of our son in a snowstorm, the parallels were eerily similar.

Packed belongings cluttered every inch of our new home, making movement and daily living a chore. But the boxes would be unpacked in time; first, I had to unpack the reality of recent events, shake off what was no longer true, and begin making a path in the newness. I learned there simply cannot be growth without purging — things and feelings.

The quiet season is not about doing, but about being. In the six months that followed our arrival in Wyoming — the same length of time it took Lee to finally unveil his true self to me all those years ago — I took baths in the middle of the day, napped on the couch and read more often than I did the dishes, cooked dinner or even got dressed during the day. I was healing deeply. With each crying bout and personal hibernation, I was slowly forming a new version of myself. I was assimilating. I had to get comfortable with the fact that I no longer had a dad who would call me weekly. I had to make peace with leaving sunny California and moving back to the rural, wintery landscape of Wyoming, where friends I once knew well had learned to live without me. All I could do was surrender and continually create new perspectives. Such deep work can be tiring. Sometimes it can be downright ugly.

The acceptance of my new normal was incremental and, like creating a massive painting, painstakingly done one deliberate brushstroke at a time. Eventually, the strokes came together and created something sensible out of nothing. It's quite like that, the quiet season. It is the shedding of an old, comfy coat that can no longer be worn. You must lay it down while figuring out how to be warm again.

Lee instinctively knew about quiet seasons. He was tender and gentle with me, aware that I was now the one with big feelings. He hugged me more and asked frequently if I was okay. He wanted to know if he could do anything, and when he couldn't, he kissed me gently as he left me to my metamorphosis.

That is what you do when you live through a quiet season. You create something completely new that will one day feel as comfortable as the coat you discarded. There is very little to be done as the newness forms around you. There is only need for surrender, for quiet, for crying and allowance, whether it is in you or in others. But despite your uncertainty, the coat will come to fit you. In time, it will even become comfortable.

You will be warm again and you will awaken to deep strength and renewal. Like a bear out of hibernation, you will stretch towards the sky and amble into the sun.

There will be a new season.

Conclusion

Everyone has a story, and the power of our stories lies in the telling. What we tell ourselves about our life stories shapes the way we look at the world and how we feel about our place in it. I'm still learning to assimilate my own story about being an adoptive mother to a child who has faced adversities I will never truly know. My son will probably spend years understanding the complexities of his story: losing his first two families, being adopted into an interracial family, growing up in a different culture, and grappling with social and learning difficulties. It's hard to watch as he wrestles with it all.

When I let myself dwell on my sadness over the past or my fears for the future, I miss all the joys and small victories of today, and there are many. From the snowy day twelve years ago when we were literally handed a toddler in the airport, I am in awe of all that we have accomplished together, what I have learned and who each of us has become in this time.

Often, we hear how lucky Lee is to have us as parents. Movies, books and church sponsorship programs subtly perpetuate the heroic idea that taking in an orphan or raising a foster child or stepchild from a tough past is about saving the child. That isn't particularly true. You see, I am the lucky one, because Lee allowed me to become a mom in a very special way. Through this epic experience, one I continue to learn from every day, I have been changed for the better. I have become my own version of a mother, a scientist, a counselor, a teacher, a student, a guide and a ninja.

I feel profoundly that I share this journey with a woman I have never met who lives halfway around the world. A woman who sent her child to me with the selfless belief that I could do better. During particularly tough parenting moments, I have often thought, *What if she could peek through a magical lens and see us at this very moment?* Thinking those thoughts felt disheartening to me. I wanted to be perfect, to smile all the time, to be the perpetual earth mother, while turning Lee into perfection, too. I wanted her to know she was right to trust me. I wanted to show her that everything would turn out the way she had hoped.

I spent many of my son's early years fretting and exhausted, trying to control the uncontrollable. I tried so hard to be the epitome of what I thought I had to be, and to make everything better when it wasn't as I imagined. On my parenting journey I have confronted deep trenches of grief, listened to the primal screams of night terrors, and hugged a child in the midst of rage, knowing it wasn't about me but about a deep well of pain I will never know. I have learned about brain development, assessed and managed school interventions, acquired new parenting techniques, consulted with counselors, and tried things that may or may not have been a version of voodoo.

I have done everything I knew to do. I have even tried to fix him. But I grow more and more confident that I am really fixing myself. He has taught me everything I know by challenging me, being resilient and utterly forgiving to a mom who still has a lot to learn.

It hasn't been easy, dear reader, but we are making it. And I know you'll make it too.

This is my mothering manifesto.

And I would not change a thing.

Resources

Adverse Experiences. (2013). Retrieved June 20, 2015, from http://www.childtrends.org/? indicators=adverse-experiences

Best, D. (Director) (2009, October 1). Therapeutic Parenting for Traumatized Children. *Creating Loving Families*. Lecture conducted from Adoption and Attachment Treatment Center of Iowa.

Cameron, J. (Director) (2014, March 31). How Toxic Stress Impacts Children's Developing Brains. Lecture conducted from YouTube.

Goewey, D. (n.d.). Stress, the Brain and the Neuroscience of Success. Retrieved July 8, 2015, from http://www.huffingtonpost.com/don-joseph-goewey-/stress-success_b_5652874.html

Harris, N. (2014, January 11). The Chronic Stress of Poverty: Toxic to Children. Retrieved May 20, 2015.

Harris, N. B. (Director) (2014, September 1). How Childhood Trauma Effects Health Across a Lifetime. *TedTalk*. Lecture conducted from Tedmed.

Hughes, Daniel A. (2006), *Building the Bonds of Attachment; Awakening Love in Deeply Troubled Children*. Maryland, Roman & Littlefield Publishers.

Palacios, J., Román, M., & Camacho, C. (2011). Growth and development in internationally adopted children: Extent and timing of recovery after early adversity. *Child: Care, Health and Development,* 282–288.

Stevens, J. (2012, December 8). The Adverse Childhood
Experiences Study — the Largest Public Health Study You
Never Heard Of, Part Three. Retrieved July 10, 2015, from
http://www.huffingtonpost.com/jane-ellen-stevens/the-
adverse-childhood-exp_7_b_1944199.html

The Enduring Effects Of Abuse And Related Adverse Experiences
In Childhood. A Convergence Of Evidence From Neurobiology
And Epidemiology. (n.d.). *Child: Care, Health and Development,*
253–256.

The Neurological Legacy of Childhood Trauma — Speaking
of Medicine. (2012, June 1). Retrieved May 20, 2015, from
http://blogs.plos.org/speakingofmedicine/2012/06/01/the-
neurological-legacy-of-childhood-trauma/

Thomas, N. (Families By Design) (2008, February 7). Children
with Reactive Attachment Disorder. Lecture conducted from
Parent Information Center, Buffalo WY.

Acknowledgements

Writing this is difficult, because I don't want to forget or slight all of the many people in my life who have made me who I am. Each family member, relative, friend and teacher have had a huge impact on me. Please know that your presence in my life is significant.

While I have had the notion to write a book for a few years, the actual writing cannot happen without the direct support of many. Above all, I would like to thank those moms who have met with me at coffee shops or in my living room and bravely told me their own stories. They were the inspiration and impetus for me to publically share my personal story. We are not alone!

I am also very grateful to my husband, who threatened to send me to a tropical island all by myself so that I could get this book written! He knows that the lure of my family is strong and I often will distract myself with caring for my son and hanging out with the family. He was absolutely diligent in orchestrating stretches of guilt free time for me to write and finish this book. Because of his unparalleled work ethic that supports our family, and his unwavering passion to be the best dad, I am free to pursue my dreams (which can be lofty and expensive!). He believes in me far more than I believe in myself.

I would be amiss if I didn't give proper accolades to all of those who helped me finish and polish this story. Julie Terhune scoured articles, compiled resources and wrote the bibliography. She also came to my house and listened to me drone on about all kinds of boring topics related to challenging behaviors. She doesn't even have kids! She deserves more than the tea and cookies I offered. Her willingness to do something she had never done before was a true gift!

Kate Makled talked me off a ledge more than once with her wise coaching and was instrumental in convincing me that telling my story was more powerful than keeping it to myself. Her tireless reading of manuscripts and thoughtful developmental input were paramount to shaping my written words. Thank you, Kate.

And I am truly indebted to my tribemate and friend, Amy Kathryn Pryce. Amy and I traipsed through France together, where our friendship blossomed. As a friend, she Skyped with me, read my manuscript almost as I many times as I did, and helped me develop a book I could be proud of despite the deadlines and mental blocks. Her ability to eloquently restructure my words while retaining the integrity of my intentions is unmatched. I am so grateful for her skills, her coaching and friendship. Thank you, Amy.

I am also thankful for every single teacher and administrator that Lee has had since Kindergarten, and I mean every single one. Each one of you has taught me something powerful. I am so grateful for the amazing and caring educators who have supported and assisted both Lee and me with unwavering dedication. To all of you who teach and toil, thank you.

Finally, to all of those who supported our family's journey from the beginning, including AAC Adoption in Berthoud, Colorado, and to those who provided their expertise along the way, especially Nina Jonio, Denise Best, and Erin McNally. Without their professional guidance and encouragement, I would have been lost. Your impact in our lives has been permanently positive.

But there is nothing like friends. To all of the strong women who walked along side me during those days when Lee was little, I am eternally grateful for your friendship.

About the Author

Wendy Borders Gauntner is an adoptive mother, educator, writer, and certified life coach who works with clients on parenting and navigating life transitions. She holds a B.A. in Education and an M.S. in Adult Learning and Technology, and is a trained community educator for Mindfulness Based Stress Reduction.

As an educator, Wendy was the first case manager in her district to develop and implement all aspects of the position. She participated in the National Teacher Policy Institute (NTPI), conducting action research on the efficacy and validity of long-term data collection and its implications for special needs students. She was also a speaker at the inaugural Wyoming Para-professional conference on fostering and maintaining a positive attitude in the workplace, has given several presentations on MBSR, and was the keynote speaker at Portage College convocation ceremony in 2014.

Wendy left her position in the school district after adopting her son in 2004. Since then, she has been a field agent for a relocation company, a Zumba© fitness instructor, and (her favorite job ever!) a background artist on TV shows such as The Mentalist, The Middle, The Client List, CSI: New York, and Brooklynn Nine-Nine. She also founded the Monday Lunch Trio Blog, where she uses recipes to illustrate life lessons and share life coaching tools. She considers herself a Life Lesson Guide, helping clients to make meaning of and give purpose to the events of their everyday lives. Wendy lives in Wyoming with her husband, son and rescue dog.

OFFER

To download FREE supplemental
worksheets related to this book,
learn more about Wendy Gauntner
or contact the author please visit:

www.WendyBorders.com| *Author Page*
www.MondayLunchTrio.com| *Blog*

difference press

Difference Press offers solopreneurs, including life coaches, healers, consultants, and community leaders, a comprehensive solution to get their books written, published, and promoted. A boutique-style alternative to self-publishing, Difference Press boasts a fair and easy-to-understand profit structure, low-priced author copies, and author-friendly contract terms. Its founder, Dr. Angela Lauria, has been bringing to life the literary ventures of hundreds of authors -in-transformation since 1994.

YOUR DELICIOUS BOOK

Your Delicious Book is a trailblazing program for aspiring authors who want to create a non-fiction book that becomes a platform for growing their business or communicating their message to the world in a way that creates a difference in the lives of others.

In a market where hundreds of thousands books are published every year and never heard from again, all of The Author Incubator participants have bestsellers that are actively changing lives and making a difference. The program, supported by quarterly Difference Press book-marketing summits, has a proven track record of helping aspiring authors write books that matter. Our team will hold your hand from idea to impact, showing you how to write a book, what elements must be present in your book for it to deliver the results you need, and how to meet the needs of your readers. We give you all the editing, design, and technical support you need to ensure a high-quality book published to the Kindle platform. Plus, authors in the program are connected to a powerful community of authors-in-transformation and published bestselling authors.

TACKLING THE TECHNICAL ASPECTS OF PUBLISHING

The comprehensive coaching, editing, design, publishing, and marketing services offered by Difference Press mean that your book will be edited by a pro, designed by an experienced graphic artist, and published digitally and in print by publishing industry experts. We handle all of the technical aspects of your book's creation so you can spend more of your time focusing on your business.

APPLY TO WRITE WITH US

To submit an application to our acquisitions team visit www.YourDeliciousBook.com.

OTHER BOOKS BY DIFFERENCE PRESS

Confessions of an Unlikely Runner: A Guide to Racing and Obstacle Courses for the Averagely Fit and Halfway Dedicated

by Dana L. Ayers

Matter: How to Find Meaningful Work That's Right for You and Your Family

by Caroline Greene

Reclaiming Wholeness: Letting Your Light Shine Even If You're Scared to Be Seen

by Kimberlie Chenoweth

The Well-Crafted Mom: How to Make Time for Yourself and Your Creativity within the Midst of Motherhood

by Kathleen Harper

Lifestyle Design for a Champagne Life: Find Out Why the Law of Attraction Isn't Working. Learn the Secret to Lifestyle Design, and Create Your Champagne Life

by Cassie Parks

No More Drama: How to Make Peace with Your Defiant Kid

by Lisa Cavallaro

The Nurse Practitioner's Bag: Become a Healer, Make a Difference, and Create the Career of Your Dreams

by Nancy Brook

Farm Girl Leaves Home: An American Narrative of Inspiration and Transformation

by Margaret Fletcher

*Whoops! I Forgot
to Achieve My
Potential*

by Maggie
Huffman

*Only 10s: Using
Distraction to
Get the Right
Things Done*

by Mark Silverman

*The Inside Guide
to MS: How to
Survive a New
Diagnosis When
Your Whole Life
Changes (And
You Just Want to
Go Home)*

by Andrea Hanson

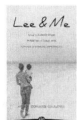

*Lee & Me:
What I Learned
from Parenting
a Child with
Adverse Childhood
Experiences*

by Wendy
Gauntner

*The Peaceful
Daughter's Guide
to Separating from
A Difficult Mother:
Freeing Yourself
From The Guilt,
Anger, Resentment
and Bitterness*

by Karen C. L.
Anderson

*Soulful Truth
Telling: Disbelieving
the Lies That Keep
Us From the
Love We Desire*

by Sharon Pope

*Personal Finance
That Doesn't Suck:
A 5-step Guide to
Quit Budgeting,
Start Wealth
Building and Get
the Most from
Your Money*

by Mindy Crary

*The Cancer
Whisperer: How
to Let Cancer
Heal Your Life*

by Sophie
Sabbage

Made in the USA
San Bernardino, CA
09 December 2015